QUIET TIMES WITH

God

DEVOTIONAL

QUIET TIMES WITH

DEVOTIONAL

365 Daily Inspirations

JOYCE MEYER

New York   Nashville

FaithWords
Hachette Book Group
1290 Avenue of the Americas, New York, NY 10104
faithwords.com
twitter.com/faithwords

First Edition: October 2020

FaithWords is a division of Hachette Book Group, Inc.
The FaithWords name and logo are trademarks of Hachette Book Group, Inc.

The publisher is not responsible for websites (or their content) that are not owned by the publisher.

The Hachette Speakers Bureau provides a wide range of authors for speaking events. To find out more, go to www.hachettespeakersbureau.com or call (866) 376-6591.

Library of Congress Cataloging-in-Publication Data has been applied for.

ISBNs: 978-1-4555-6028-8 (hardcover); 978-1-4555-6029-5 (large type), 978-1-4555-6030-1 (ebook)

Printed in the United States of America

Printing 2,2020

INTRODUCTION

Without a doubt, the very best time you can spend each day is *time with God*. No matter how hectic your schedule or how busy your day, if you slow down and spend time with God, you'll be amazed at the difference it will make.

We live in a world that seems to get louder and louder. The demands of work, the busyness of life, the distractions of social media and entertainment—these all seem to almost shout at our souls. None of these things are bad in themselves, but if we aren't careful, we can allow them to drown out the voice of God.

Keep in mind, God doesn't compete for our attention. His voice is not abrasive or overbearing. 1 Kings 19:12 gives us a picture of God speaking with "[a sound of gentle stillness and] a still, small voice" (AMPC). I think this is why so many people say they haven't heard from God. It's not that God isn't speaking to them; it's just that they haven't slowed down and quieted their souls in order to hear Him.

That's why I've titled this devotional *Quiet Times with God*. My prayer is that as you take time to pray, read and study God's Word, or just meditate on His goodness, it will enrich your life in amazing ways. I hope these devotionals will be a great starting point for you. Each devotional has a scripture, a thought to consider, and encouragements on various topics from the Word. Make spending time with God a priority in your life; it will be the best time you spend all day long!

For God alone my soul waits in silence; from Him comes my salvation.

Psalm 62:1

God Is Your Power Source

I am the Vine; you are the branches. The one who remains in Me and I in him bears much fruit, for [otherwise] apart from Me [that is, cut off from vital union with Me] you can do nothing. (John 15:5)

Your life in Christ is not a do-it-yourself project. In other words, you are not left on your own to solve your problems or meet life's challenges in your own strength. God is with you. *He* is your source.

As you grow in your personal relationship with God—spending time talking with Him and studying His Word—you progressively learn to look to God at all times, leaning on His strength rather than your own. You begin to understand that He is your unfailing provider.

Because God is always with you, you have access to everything you need to be victorious in life. Peace, joy, confidence, strength, wisdom, and all the fruit of the Spirit—it's all available to you in Christ Jesus.

Today's Thought

Instead of wondering, How am I going to get everything done? *or* How am I going to figure this problem out? *ask God for His help, strength, and guidance. Trust Him to be your source.*

Dig Deeper into God's Word: Study Isaiah 40:29;
    Ephesians 3:16

Waiting with Expectation

Wait for and confidently expect the Lord; be strong and let your heart take courage; yes, wait for and confidently expect the Lord. (Psalm 27:14)

At some point in our lives, we all find ourselves praying about a situation and waiting for God to answer that prayer. Waiting can be difficult, and we often wonder if God has heard our prayers.

But be assured, God does hear every prayer you pray, and He is working out the answers even though you may not know all the details. Until you get an answer to your prayer, you can wait either passively or expectantly.

A passive person gives up easily, but an expectant person is confident, believing the answer is just around the corner. Expectancy fills us with hope. It gives us the faith and the strength to wake up each morning with excitement: This could be the day God does something amazing!

Today's Thought

Even when you're waiting on the Lord, be active. Actively pray, actively study the Word, and actively believe that God is working, even when you can't see it.

Dig Deeper into God's Word: Study Habakkuk 2:3; Psalm 39:7

It's Going to Be a Good Day

This [day in which God has saved me] is the day which the Lord has made; let us rejoice and be glad in it. (Psalm 118:24)

Have you ever said, "Well, I'm just having a bad day"? Most of us have. But the problem with bad days is they tend to pile up. A bad day becomes a bad week. A bad week becomes a bad month. And before you know it, a bad month can become a bad year.

You don't have to go through life held hostage by your circumstances. It doesn't matter what happens *around* you; if you've accepted Jesus Christ as your Savior, you have the Spirit of God *within* you. Your hope and happiness are not dependent on the world. The Bible declares, "He who is in you is greater than he (Satan) who is in the world [of sinful mankind]" (1 John 4:4).

Sunny or raining, good report or bad, surrounded by friends or standing alone, you can enjoy every day of this life God has given you. He is with you at all times. Pause frequently throughout the day and say, "God is with me right now!"

Today's Thought

God wants you to enjoy your life every day, not just occasionally. Every day can be a wonderful day because God is on your side.

Dig Deeper into God's Word: Study John 15:11; Job 8:21

Overcoming the Impossible

I can do all things [which He has called me to do] through Him who strengthens and empowers me [to fulfill His purpose—I am self-sufficient in Christ's sufficiency; I am ready for anything and equal to anything through Him who infuses me with inner strength and confident peace.] (Philippians 4:13)

Never assume that where you've been or where you are is as good as it gets. And when your goal or your situation seems impossible, keep in mind that nothing is impossible for God. In Matthew 19:26, Jesus said, "With people [as far as it depends on them] it is impossible, but with God all things are possible."

The greatest things you can do in life are the things you can't do on your own. You know you are on the right track when a challenge or an opportunity can only be done with God's help.

It doesn't matter what the situation looks like around you; God is greater than any obstacle you may be facing. Anything that has never been done is impossible until someone does it, so why can't it be you? Don't allow your mind to become a hindrance to the things you can accomplish in life. Think big—the way God does.

Today's Thought

Believe God is going to do something better in your life. Go ahead and get your hopes up…God is leading you to something better than you can imagine.

Dig Deeper into God's Word: Study Romans 12:21;
    1 John 5:4

Faith Instead of Fear

For God did not give us a spirit of timidity or cowardice or fear, but [He has given us a spirit] of power and of love and of sound judgment and personal discipline [abilities that result in a calm, well-balanced mind and self-control]. (2 Timothy 1:7)

Fear, simply put, is the opposite of faith. God wants us to walk by faith, but Satan tries to make us live in fear. When we learn to live by faith and not let fear rule our lives, we can live a fulfilling, satisfying, peaceful, and joyful life in Christ.

Fear begins with a thought. Proverbs 23:7 tells us that "as [a man] thinks in his heart, so is he" (NKJV). I like to say it this way: Where the mind goes, the man follows.

This is why the Bible talks about meditating on the Word of God and having your mind renewed (see Romans 12:2). To meditate on God's Word means you ponder the Scripture over and over in your mind until it becomes part of you. When you do this, it takes information and turns it into revelation. The more you study God's Word and think about His promises, the better your life will be!

Today's Thought

Think about what you are thinking about. Instead of fearful or worried thoughts, choose to focus on thoughts that are full of faith.

Dig Deeper into God's Word: Study 1 John 4:18; Psalm 118:6

God's Perfect Timing

[With joy] let us exult in our sufferings and rejoice in our hardships, knowing that hardship (distress, pressure, trouble) produces patient endurance; and endurance, proven character (spiritual maturity); and proven character, hope and confident assurance [of eternal salvation]. (Romans 5:3–4)

God has a tremendous plan for each of our lives, and He wants to greatly bless us. However, He may not bless our circumstances beyond the level of our spiritual maturity.

For example, I prayed for years for my ministry to grow. But if God had given me everything I wanted before I was spiritually mature enough, it would have hurt me because I wouldn't have had the godly character and strength to handle it all. It may sound strange, but now I am so grateful for the hard times when I had to wait on God's timing, because they've helped bring me to where I am today.

When you feel like things aren't happening the *way* you want, *when* you want, I encourage you to trust God's perfect timing. He knows what you can handle, and He always has your very best interest in mind.

Today's Thought

God is preparing you for the plan He has for you.

Dig Deeper into God's Word: Study Isaiah 30:18; Ecclesiastes 3:11

Knowing Who You Are

Therefore if anyone is in Christ [that is, grafted in, joined to Him by faith in Him as Savior], he is a new creature [reborn and renewed by the Holy Spirit]; the old things [the previous moral and spiritual condition] have passed away. Behold, new things have come [because spiritual awakening brings a new life]. (2 Corinthians 5:17)

There are many people who aren't using their gifts and talents from God because they tried and failed in the past. They are frustrated in life because they have let past defeats define who they are. Instead of quitting or giving up, God wants you to keep trying until you get it right!

When we become born again through a relationship with Jesus Christ, we actually become "re-created" in Him. So whatever Jesus is, we are, too.

- He is strong, and in Him, we are strong (see Philippians 4:13).
- He is courageous; in Him, we are courageous (see Matthew 19:26; John 16:33).
- He is a conqueror, so we conquer, too (see Romans 8:37).
- He has peace and joy, so we have peace and joy (see John 14:27).

You can overcome any defeats or failures of the past by seeing yourself in Christ. Then you will find you have whatever you need in order to do what you were created to do.

Today's Thought

Your past mistakes don't have to determine your future!

Dig Deeper into God's Word: Study Genesis 1:27; Romans 8:37

Unconditional Love

But God, being [so very] rich in mercy, because of His great and wonderful love with which He loved us, even when we were [spiritually] dead and separated from Him because of our sins, He made us [spiritually] alive together with Christ (for by His grace—His undeserved favor and mercy—you have been saved from God's judgment). (Ephesians 2:4–5)

One of the most beautiful things the Bible says is that while we were still sinners, Christ died for us (see Romans 5:8). He did not wait for us to deserve His love. He loves us unconditionally.

Because of His great, wonderful, and unconditional love, God poured His life out for us freely. That is revolutionary love—real, incomprehensible love that gives itself away because it can never be satisfied doing anything less.

Never forget, it is God's unconditional love that draws us to Him, His amazing grace that erases our sin, and His powerful sacrifice that makes a way for us to enter into relationship with Him. Take time in God's presence today to simply think about how much He loves you!

Today's Thought

God's love for you is available right now, and all you need to do is receive it!

Dig Deeper into God's Word: Study John 3:16; Ephesians 3:17–19

Being a Decisive Person

*So we take comfort and are encouraged and confidently
say, "The Lord is my Helper [in time of need], I will not be
afraid. What will man do to me?" (Hebrews 13:6)*

If you've ever felt stressed out in the face of multiple options, I have
good news for you: You can be a person who makes wise, bold, and
confident decisions.

You don't have to go through life feeling indecisive and unsure,
and you don't have to be intimidated any longer by the sheer number of choices before you.

Simply ask God for His direction and then take the steps He
gives you peace about. When you trust His guidance, He will show
you what decision to make. Believe that you have God's wisdom,
and take steps of faith rather than being frozen in fear!

Today's Thought

*You can hear from God, and you can be led and guided by
the Holy Spirit. Believe it and be confident!*

Dig Deeper into God's Word: Study James 1:5;
    Psalm 49:3

Find the Good in Everything

Let no corrupt word proceed out of your mouth, but what is good for necessary edification, that it may impart grace to the hearers. (Ephesians 4:29 NKJV)

There is great strength in speaking positive, faith-filled words over your day. Rather than talking about all the things you're dreading, speak God's promises over the day to come, and incredible things can happen.

- Instead of saying, "Ugh, it looks like rain today. How depressing," say something like, "Rain or shine, I'm going to have a great day!"
- Instead of saying, "I have so much work to do this week. I can't wait until it's over," say something like, "It looks like a challenging week ahead, but I can't wait to see how God is going to use me!"

Do you see the difference? When you change the conversation, you stop dread dead in its tracks. Speak confident, optimistic words each day and watch what God will do!

Today's Thought

Have the faith to speak about God's promises; that opens the door for Him to work in your life.

Dig Deeper into God's Word: Study Nahum 1:7;
        Proverbs 18:21

Living in the Now

Now may the Lord of peace Himself grant you His peace at all times and in every way [that peace and spiritual well-being that comes to those who walk with Him, regardless of life's circumstances]. (2 Thessalonians 3:16)

Having an attitude of peace and calm is priceless. It's an attitude that says, "I'm trusting God," and it honors Him and speaks powerfully to others.

One way to develop consistent peace is to learn to live "in the now." We can spend a lot of time thinking about the past or wondering what the future holds...but we can't accomplish anything unless our mind is focused on today.

The Bible tells us that God gives us grace for each day that we live; He doesn't give it to us before we need it. I believe that grace is the power, enablement, or energy to do what we need to do—and He gives it generously. Your power and ability will increase if you focus on what you are doing instead of allowing your mind to worry about the past or the future.

Today's Thought

You can make a decision every morning to say, "God has given me today. I will rejoice and live each moment as it comes!"

Dig Deeper into God's Word: Study Matthew 6:34;
Psalm 16:5

Walking Out God's Perfect Plan

A man's mind plans his way [as he journeys through life], but the Lord directs his steps and establishes them. (Proverbs 16:9)

We think and plan in temporal terms, but God thinks and plans in infinite terms. What this means is that we are very interested in right now, and God is much more interested in eternity.

Never forget that God sees and understands what we can't yet see or understand. He asks us to trust Him, not to live in frustration because things don't always go according to our plan. He wants us to trust that He is working His perfect plan . . . in His perfect timing.

We often want what produces immediate results, but God is willing to invest time. God is an investor; He invests time in us, and if we choose to invest time in and with Him, we will love the result!

Today's Thought

Not only does God have a plan for your life, but He has the perfect timing for each step of that wonderful plan.

Dig Deeper into God's Word: Study Ecclesiastes 3:1; Psalm 37:4–7

Discipline Leads to Joy

Rather, he must be hospitable, one who loves what is good, who is self-controlled, upright, holy and disciplined. (Titus 1:8 NIV)

There are many things that compete for our limited amount of time and energy. These things often steal our joy.

I used to complain to God about my schedule being too busy. I'd say, "God, how could anyone be expected to do all that I have to do?" Then God showed me that I was the one who made my schedule and nobody could change it but me. God showed me that simplifying my schedule was the way to simplify my life.

Ask God to show you what changes you can make to eliminate the stress of rushing, and then discipline yourself to make those changes. Spend time with God first, and you will find that the remainder of your time will be more fruitful and peaceful.

Today's Thought

Decide today that you are going to manage your schedule instead of allowing it to manage you.

Dig Deeper into God's Word: Study Proverbs 1:7;
    Hebrews 12:7

Something Good Is Going to Happen!

But those who wait for the Lord [who expect, look for, and hope in Him] will gain new strength and renew their power. (Isaiah 40:31)

Hope is a positive expectation that something good is going to happen because of God's great love for you. It is not a wishy-washy, wait-and-see attitude, but a mindset we must choose on purpose each day.

Hope in Christ enables us to endure hardships and long waiting periods without giving up, and God uses these times to develop character and endurance in us.

Hope reminds us to believe that God has a plan; things are going to work out. It is the sometimes unexplainable but always undeniable feeling that today would be a bad day to give up. When you choose hope, you are choosing to keep moving forward, knowing that God will make a way.

Today's Thought

When facing a difficult day or a tough situation, choose hope over despair or discouragement. God is in control!

Dig Deeper into God's Word: Study Psalm 5:3; Jude 1:21

Jesus Has Overcome

I have told you these things, so that in Me you may have [perfect] peace. In the world you have tribulation and distress and suffering, but be courageous [be confident, be undaunted, be filled with joy]; I have overcome the world. (John 16:33)

Too often, our stress level is tied to our circumstances. We could be stressed because we're always busy, we're struggling financially, or we're not getting along with someone we love.

It could be a number of things, but what's interesting is that these situations are not actually the cause of stress. Stress is *really* caused by our perspective of our circumstances.

If we focus on our blessings instead of our challenges, then the challenges won't seem so daunting. Jesus said we would have tribulation, but He also promised us victory. Instead of letting problems make us miserable, we can cheer up! No matter what is happening right now, we will win in the end.

Today's Thought

When the storms of life rage around you, trust that God is going to carry you through the storm and bring you safely to the other side.

Dig Deeper into God's Word: Study 1 Corinthians 15:57; John 1:5

Closeness with Your Heavenly Father

For you have not received a spirit of slavery leading again to fear [of God's judgment], but you have received the Spirit of adoption as sons [the Spirit producing sonship] by which we [joyfully] cry, "Abba! Father!" (Romans 8:15)

Abba was a term used by little children in addressing their father. It would be similar to the word *Daddy* today. This term is less formal than *father* and denotes a comfortable closeness between a child and their father.

Jesus said that we could call God Abba because He had delivered us from all fear. He will always take care of His beloved children, and we can approach Him without any fear of rejection or condemnation.

When we run to our Heavenly Father—our Abba—with any problem or pain, He is waiting with open arms to comfort and encourage us.

Today's Thought

God is not a distant, far-off, out-of-touch God. He loves you deeply, and He wants to have a close, personal relationship with you.

Dig Deeper into God's Word: Study Galatians 4:6;
    Romans 8:1

Moving Past Pain

*Bearing graciously with one another, and willingly for-
giving each other if one has a cause for complaint against
another; just as the Lord has forgiven you, so should you
forgive. (Colossians 3:13)*

Being hurt or betrayed by someone close to you—someone you
love—is one of the most painful and difficult situations you will
ever endure, but if it happens, you must let God heal you and move
beyond it, or it will destroy you. Without forgiveness, you will simply be alone with your pain, bitterness, and resentment. In addi-
tion, your ability to enjoy God and His good plan for you will be
diminished, if not entirely destroyed.

Do yourself a favor and totally forgive the person who hurt you.
God never asks you to do anything without giving you the ability
to do it. With His help, you can forgive and move past your pain.
You don't have to spend your life feeling hurt, bitter, angry, and
offended. You can forgive and be free.

Today's Thought

*When you forgive, you think you're letting someone out of
prison. Only after forgiveness do you realize that the prisoner was you.*

Dig Deeper into God's Word: Study Psalm 32:10;
     Revelation 21:4

God Knows Everything about You ... and He Loves You

O Lord, you have searched me [thoroughly] and have known me. (Psalm 139:1)

In order to be in a close relationship with God, it is important to know that He is pleased with you, in spite of your perceived flaws and imperfections.

Many people suffer terribly with secret worries that they are not pleasing to God. They are afraid that God is angry with them because of the mistakes they have made.

But the truth is that you are righteous through the work of Jesus, not through your own works. You are imperfect, you will make mistakes, and God is not surprised when you do. He knew every mistake you would ever make when He called you into relationship with Himself.

Psalm 139 tells us plainly that God knows what we are going to do before we ever do it, so try to keep in mind that God knows *all* about you, and He loves you anyway.

Today's Thought

If you could be perfect on your own, you would not need Jesus.

Dig Deeper into God's Word: Study Romans 8:38–39;
    1 John 4:16

Three Ways to Practice Peace

You will keep in perfect and constant peace the one whose mind is steadfast [that is, committed and focused on You—in both inclination and character], because he trusts and takes refuge in You [with hope and confident expectation]. (Isaiah 26:3)

I believe that one of the keys to maintaining peace in your life is to take small steps toward peace every day. Here are three tips for having a more peaceful lifestyle.

1. *Be selective with how you spend your time.* You may be trying to do too many things and end up doing none of them well. *Hurrying* is trying to do more than the Holy Spirit is leading you to do—slow down and be led by the Holy Spirit.

2. *Set boundaries for yourself.* Life is full of interruptions, but we can learn to set boundaries that help us manage them in healthy ways instead of letting them control us. Schedule times when you are off-limits. Let your calls go to voice mail, turn off your email, learn to say no, and so on.

3. *Listen for the Holy Spirit.* If you can see that your plan is not producing peace, go back to God to find the source of the problem and make changes that will allow you to enjoy a peaceful life.

Today's Thought

If you can learn to schedule your day wisely and follow the Holy Spirit's guidance throughout your week, you can become a truly peaceful person.

Dig Deeper into God's Word: Study Matthew 5:9; Colossians 3:15

Plugging into Grace with Faith

Now faith is the assurance (title deed, confirmation) of things hoped for (divinely guaranteed), and the evidence of things not seen [the conviction of their reality—faith comprehends as fact what cannot be experienced by the physical senses]. (Hebrews 11:1)

Faith is how we plug in to the grace of God. Think of it like a lamp: The lamp can only give light if it is plugged in to a power source. If it's unplugged, it will not work, no matter how many times we turn the switch on and off.

So let me ask you: Are you plugged in to God's power, or are you unplugged? Have you let fear and worry creep into your soul? Are you attempting to solve your problems in your own power, or do you have faith that God's power, His grace, will bring you through to victory?

You can regain your peace right now by simply releasing your faith in God and trusting Him to do what needs to be done in your life.

Today's Thought

Grace is received only through faith. That is why it is so important to do all that we do in faith.

Dig Deeper into God's Word: Study Ephesians 2:8; Galatians 2:16

Strength in Perseverance

Let us not grow weary or become discouraged in doing good, for at the proper time we will reap, if we do not give in. (Galatians 6:9)

One of the most important traits a person can have is persistent determination. A persistent person is prepared and powerful. They have determined that they will not give up until they succeed.

Persistence is key, because there are going to be difficulties in life. The Bible never promised that when you gave your life to God, you'd no longer have any problems. As I'm sure you've noticed, life isn't always easy. There are going to be difficult days and trying circumstances, but going *through* them instead of giving up is what makes us strong.

The Bible gives us many examples of perseverance to follow. Moses didn't give up when he faced Egyptian opposition. Esther didn't give up in her plan to save her people. David didn't give up when Saul attacked him. And Paul didn't give up even when he was jailed for preaching the gospel.

These examples teach us that when we know who we are in God and trust His work in our lives, we won't give up, no matter how challenging life is. When things get tough, persevere through the strength you have in Christ.

Today's Thought

Make a decision that you will never, never, never give up!

Dig Deeper into God's Word: Study Hebrews 6:12; Matthew 24:13

Resisting the Enemy

So submit to [the authority of] God. Resist the devil [stand firm against him] and he will flee from you. (James 4:7)

Though you do have an enemy, you have nothing to fear. The devil has no power over you...none! The moment you gave your life to the Lord, you became a redeemed, forgiven, righteous child of God. Satan has no rightful place in your life, so don't let him deceive you.

Rather than living in fear, you can be empowered by God, through faith, to live a bold, productive life that is filled with happiness and the power of God.

You don't ever have to live in worry or doubt, wondering, *Is the enemy going to defeat me today?* The Spirit of God in you is greater than any attack of the devil. The Bible gives you this assurance: "He who is in you is greater than he (Satan) who is in the world [of sinful mankind]" (1 John 4:4).

Today's Thought

Refuse to live with a defeated mindset. You are a victor! An overcomer! More than a conqueror!

Dig Deeper into God's Word: Study Psalm 1:1; 2 Chronicles 7:14

The Armor of God
Provided for You

Be strong in the Lord [draw your strength from Him and be empowered through your union with Him] and in the power of His [boundless] might. (Ephesians 6:10)

The apostle Paul teaches in the book of Ephesians that you are equipped with the "armor of God" so that you can "draw your strength from Him." He goes on to say that this armor of God will allow you to "stand your ground" (see Ephesians 6:10–13).

In Christ, you are a warrior, with access to all the armor you need to defeat the enemy in every area of your life. You have been given:

- The belt of truth (living in the truth of Scripture)
- The breastplate of righteousness (knowing you have right standing with God because of Jesus)
- The shoes of peace (walking in the peace of God)
- The shield of faith (believing God's promises)
- The helmet of salvation (hope that accompanies your salvation)
- The sword of the Spirit (speaking the Word of God)

Now, put on the full armor of God and stand strong!

Today's Thought

You are stronger than you think you are! You can do whatever you need to do with God's help.

Dig Deeper into God's Word: Study Ephesians 6:14–18; Romans 13:12

How to Put on the Armor of God

Therefore, put on the complete armor of God, so that you will be able to [successfully] resist and stand your ground in the evil day [of danger], and having done everything [that the crisis demands], to stand firm [in your place, fully prepared, immovable, victorious]. (Ephesians 6:13)

The Bible says that you must *put on* the armor God has given you—this is a conscious decision on your part. The daily decisions you make and the words you say are how you actively dress yourself in God's armor. Take a few minutes in prayer every morning and say, *Lord, today I put on the armor You have provided me through Jesus. I thank You that I am righteous today in Christ. I choose to wear the breastplate of righteousness. And I thank You that I have the shield of faith. Today I will choose to live by faith not by sight, trusting the promises in Your Word. Also, I thank You that You have armed me with the sword of the Spirit.*

Then go through the list of armor found in Ephesians 6:13–17, piece by piece. Confessing these promises out loud helps renew your mind and release the blessings of God that are yours, and it reminds the devil you know your rights as a child of God.

Today's Thought

Confessing God's Word is one of the ways you release your faith to work on your behalf.

Dig Deeper into God's Word: Study 1 Thessalonians 5:8; 2 Corinthians 10:4

Righteousness, Peace, and Joy

For the kingdom of God is not a matter of eating and drinking [what one likes], but of righteousness and peace and joy in the Holy Spirit. (Romans 14:17)

As soon as you accept Christ, His love is poured into your heart. In fact, He loved you before you ever accepted Him as your Savior.

The promise that God loves you is one of the most important truths you will ever know. Receiving God's love, loving Him in return, and then loving yourself in a healthy, balanced way is the first step toward fulfilling your destiny. Become a vessel of God's love so you can spread His love to others. It is the key to having everything that Jesus died for you to have.

Romans 14:17 tells us that the kingdom of God is not food or drink. It is much more than "things"; it is something much more important—it is His righteousness, peace, and joy.

Today's Thought

When you understand God's love for you, you can accept that you have right standing with Him, you can let go of fear and worry, and you can enjoy the life Jesus came to give you.

Dig Deeper into God's Word: Study Proverbs 21:21; 2 Corinthians 13:11

A Fresh Start

And I will compensate you for the years that the swarming locust has eaten…You will have plenty to eat and be satisfied and praise the name of the Lord your God who has dealt wondrously with you; and My people shall never be put to shame. (Joel 2:25–26)

All throughout Scripture, God forgave, redeemed, and used regular people in mighty ways. Our God is the God of do-overs, second chances, fresh starts, and new beginnings.

Maybe you're stuck, frozen in a moment. It could be a personal failure of some kind or something completely beyond your control, like an illness or the death of a loved one. Perhaps you've been disappointed by an unmet expectation—things didn't turn out the way you wanted them to. So you think, *It's over. It's too late for me.*

But it isn't too late. It's never too late to have a fresh start when you have Jesus in your life. Your past is not your destiny. If you refuse to give up hope and you make a fresh start, not only will God restore what you may have lost, He will make your life even better.

Today's Thought

The pain of your past cannot stop God's great plan for your future.

Dig Deeper into God's Word: Study Psalm 80:3; 1 Peter 5:10

Embracing Hope

May the God of hope fill you with all joy and peace in believing [through the experience of your faith] that by the power of the Holy Spirit you will abound in hope and overflow with confidence in His promises. (Romans 15:13)

Regardless of who you are or what condition your life is in, you can't function successfully without hope in God. If circumstances are bad, you surely need hope, and if they are good, you need hope that they will stay that way.

Hope energizes and motivates us to take action by causing us to step out in faith and act in obedience to God's Word. Hope believes boldly, decides daringly, speaks firmly, and perseveres passionately. Hope expects something good to happen!

When we embrace hope on purpose, it influences our thoughts, our outlook, and the way we speak. Hope builds us up as we wait on God. It releases joy, and the joy of the Lord becomes our source of strength (see Nehemiah 8:10).

Today's Thought

Dare to hope! Dare to dream! Dare to expect something wonderful to happen to you!

Dig Deeper into God's Word: Study Hebrews 6:19; 1
     Peter 1:3

Pull the Weed before It Takes Root

Having been deeply rooted [in Him] and now being continually built up in Him and [becoming increasingly more] established in your faith, just as you were taught, and overflowing in it with gratitude. (Colossians 2:7)

There are good seeds and bad ones, things we do and do not want to get rooted in our lives.

When a seed is planted, it takes a while before it has long, strong roots. Should the seed be dug up and discarded before it has opportunity to take root, there would never be any fruit from it.

When we experience a thought, an emotion, a behavior, or a fear that we don't want to become a permanent fixture, the best thing to do is resist it at its onset. Be aggressive in confronting it and firm in your decision not to give in to it. Always remember that the longer you let something linger, the longer it will take to get rid of it.

Today's Thought

Don't merely submit to a negative emotion without a fight, but when you fight, always remember to fight in God's power and not your own.

Dig Deeper into God's Word: Study Matthew 13:37–39; Galatians 3:29

Love That Is Freely Offered

For You, O Lord, are good, and ready to forgive [our sins, sending them away, completely letting them go forever and ever]; and abundant in lovingkindness and overflowing in mercy to all those who call upon You. (Psalm 86:5)

In our relationships with our parents or others, we may have had to perform in a certain way in order to earn their love, but God's love is not like that. His love is freely offered to all who receive it by faith.

Though God does get angry at sin, wickedness, and evil, He is not an angry God. God hates sin, but He loves sinners! He is "good, and ready to forgive." He is abundant in mercy and filled with loving-kindness.

God will never give up on us, and He will continue to work with us toward positive change in our lives. God never stops loving us for even one second. He meets us right where we are and helps us get to where we need to be.

Today's Thought

It is because of God's great love that He refuses to leave us alone, lost and abandoned in sin.

Dig Deeper into God's Word: Study Psalm 33:5;
   Jeremiah 31:3

Why Am I Having Problems?

Beloved, do not be surprised at the fiery ordeal which is taking place to test you [that is, to test the quality of your faith], as though something strange or unusual were happening to you. (1 Peter 4:12)

One reason we go through trials is to test the quality of our faith. Often, we find ourselves wishing we had faith as strong as another person. I can assure you, if that person has a strong and vibrant faith, they did not develop it easily. Just as muscles are built through exercise, firm faith comes from the furnace of affliction.

No one who does anything worthwhile for God has traveled an easy road. Doing great things for God requires character, and character is developed by passing life's tests and staying faithful to Him through trials.

The next time you encounter some sort of test or trial, determine to believe God will work it out for your good. Pass the test and trust God to promote you to new levels of power and blessing!

Today's Thought

Instead of asking why you are having trials, ask God to help you have a right response to them.

Dig Deeper into God's Word: Study 1 Peter 1:6;
James 1:12

Fellowship with God

In the night my soul longs for You [O Lord], indeed, my spirit within me seeks You diligently; for [only] when Your judgments are experienced on the earth will the inhabitants of the world learn righteousness. (Isaiah 26:9)

Nothing can satisfy our longing for God except communion and fellowship with Him. Isaiah expressed well our own hunger for God when he wrote, "In the night my soul longs for You [O Lord], indeed my spirit within me seeks You diligently." Isaiah needed quiet times with God, and so do we.

Hearing from God is vital to enjoying His eternal plan for our lives. Listening to God is our decision; no one else can make it for us. God won't force us to choose His will, but He will do everything He can to encourage us to say yes to His ways.

This means God wants to be involved in even the smallest details of our lives. His Word tells us to acknowledge Him in all our ways, and He will direct our paths (see Proverbs 3:6). To acknowledge God is to care what He thinks and to ask for His opinion. If you do this on a daily basis, you'll find His guidance and walk in a much closer relationship with Him.

Today's Thought

God is always speaking. The question is, are you listening?

Dig Deeper into God's Word: Study 1 John 1:3; 1 Corinthians 1:9

Be Yourself

I will praise You, for I am fearfully and wonderfully made; marvelous are Your works, and that my soul knows very well. (Psalm 139:14 NKJV)

In order to overcome insecurities and be the person God has called you to be, it is important to have the courage to be different. Unhappiness and frustration happen when we reject our uniqueness and try to be like other people.

God wants you to like and accept the person He created you to be, rather than trying to live up to other people's expectations or be what you think they want you to be. You must ask yourself, *Am I a people-pleaser or a God-pleaser?* Real peace and joy in life come when we focus on pleasing God, not man.

God knew what He was doing when He made you. You are a unique individual—fearfully and wonderfully made by Him!

Today's Thought

Accept yourself as a new creation in Christ Jesus, and gain security and confidence by discovering who you are in Him.

Dig Deeper into God's Word: Study Ephesians 4:24; Psalm 139:13

Is Jesus Your Number One Priority?

And He Himself existed and is before all things, and in Him all things hold together. [His is the controlling, cohesive force of the universe.] (Colossians 1:17)

Colossians 1:17 tells us that Jesus is holding everything together. What an amazing truth. Think about it. We can't have good marriages or friendships if Jesus isn't holding them together. Nothing works right without Jesus, so be sure that you invite Him into everything you do.

If Jesus is not the most important thing in our lives, then we need to rearrange our priorities. Matthew 6:33 tells us to seek God and His kingdom first, because if we don't have first things first, then everything else will be out of order and cause us problems. If you have not done so yet, then start today giving Jesus first place in your life.

Today's Thought

When you reprioritize your life, putting Jesus at the top of the list, you'll be amazed at how everything else will come together for your good.

Dig Deeper into God's Word: Study Mark 12:30; Numbers 15:41

A Positive Mind Yields Powerful Results

For with God nothing [is or ever] shall be impossible.
(Luke 1:37)

Having a positive mindset goes beyond the proverbial idea of simply seeing a glass as half full rather than half empty. It extends to making decisions and taking action based on hope-filled thinking.

Have you ever noticed how negative thinking blows a problem way out of proportion? Situations begin to seem larger and more difficult than they really are.

Meditate on God's Word and let it renew your mind so you can think like God thinks. Practice being positive at all times and you will have a new joy. There is great power available to us through God when we choose to trust Him in every circumstance. A positive mindset based on God's Word knows that nothing is too big for God. He is always present, and nothing is impossible with Him.

Today's Thought

No matter how many negative things and people surround you, be positive and expect good things.

Dig Deeper into God's Word: Study Matthew 19:26;
    Matthew 15:11

Your Relationship with You

You shall love your neighbor as yourself [that is, unselfishly seek the best or higher good for others]. (Matthew 22:39)

We all understand that we have relationships with other people, but did it ever occur to you that you have a relationship with yourself? Think about it: You spend more time with yourself than anyone else. So let me ask you a question: *How is your relationship with you?*

We can come to a place where we love and value ourselves, not out of pride or arrogance, but out of confidence in who we are in Christ. This understanding is the key to embracing the person you were created to be.

We can learn to become spiritually mature enough to understand that even when God shows us a change that is needed in us, He is doing it because He loves us and wants the best for us. We can say, "I believe God is changing me daily, but during this process, I will not devalue what God values. I'll accept myself because God accepts me."

Today's Thought

As you begin to see yourself as God sees you—as someone who's valued and cherished—your view of yourself will begin to change. You'll see yourself as a person who is worth investing in.

Dig Deeper into God's Word: Study Psalm 139:16; 1 John 3:1

How to Invest in Yourself

Do you not know that your body is a temple of the Holy Spirit who is within you, whom you have [received as a gift] from God, and that you are not your own [property]?...So then, honor and glorify God with your body. (1 Corinthians 6:19–20)

Once you begin to see how valuable and precious you are to God, you will begin to understand the importance in investing in yourself. Let me show you a few specific ways you can do that.

- *Decide to get some daily exercise.* However you choose to exercise—walking, jogging, swimming, lifting weights—make a plan and stick to it.
- *Get the proper amount of sleep.* Adequate rest is crucial in taking care of your body.
- *Nurture and develop your mind.* Read books, be creative, keep your brain active. Find ways to stimulate your mind and increase your learning.
- *Begin a new healthy habit.* The best way to quit bad habits is to start good habits!
- *Pursue your skills and develop your talents.* Find the things you are naturally good at, spend time practicing them, and get even better.

These are just a few of the many ways you can invest in yourself.

Today's Thought

A good investment in yourself always pays off in the long run. God wants you to invest in you!

Dig Deeper into God's Word: Study Proverbs 3:7–8; Nehemiah 8:10

Don't Get ahead of God

I will instruct you and teach you in the way you should go;
I will counsel you [who are willing to learn] with My eye
upon you. (Psalm 32:8)

God has His own timing. He may drop a dream, vision, or idea
in your heart at one point in your life and then not ask you to do
anything about it for years. Moses underwent a forty-year training
period in the desert before he was prepared to fulfill God's call on
his life. Even though God has prepared something for you to do, He
may still need to prepare you so you can do it successfully.

I hope you do not have to wait that long, but no matter what the
time frame is, just be patient. Resist the urge to get out in front of
God, and don't allow yourself to lag behind Him. Trying to move
outside of His timing—either too quickly or too slowly—will cause
you the kind of frustration that makes you want to give up, because
His presence will not be there. But when you patiently move in His
timing, as He directs, there is nothing that can stop His plan for
your life!

Today's Thought

Whether God asks you to wait two weeks or two years, be
sensitive to His timing in your life and be willing to wait
for Him as He leads you into the new place He has for you.

Dig Deeper into God's Word: Study Micah 6:8;
     Ecclesiastes 3:1–4

The Power of Laughter

A happy heart is good medicine and a joyful mind causes heal-
ing, but a broken spirit dries up the bones. (Proverbs 17:22)

God has given us the ability to laugh for a reason. It may seem like
a little thing, but laughter is vitally important in the battle against
stress, anxiety, fear, and worry. It's a tool from God that benefits
you in so many ways.

The Word of God says that a happy heart is good medicine. It
is good because laughter lifts your spirits; improves your mental,
emotional, and physical health; and destresses your mind. And
here is the best part: It costs nothing, and it is a lot of fun!

Pray that God will bring more laughter into your life, and be
sure to take advantage of any opportunity He gives you.

Today's Thought

It doesn't matter if it's a night of extreme laughter with
hilarious friends, the enjoyment of a funny movie with your
family, or even just a giggle over a silly joke—all laughter
is a form of stress relief.

Dig Deeper into God's Word: Study Proverbs 31:25;
Psalm 4:7

The Best Kind of Confidence

You need not fight in this battle; take your positions, stand and witness the salvation of the Lord who is with you. (2 Chronicles 20:17)

Confidence is an essential key to enjoying your life. When you live with confidence, worry and discouragement have little to no effect on you.

But I'm not talking about self-confidence. Self-confidence may be helpful to have, but even the most self-confident person has their limitations. The kind of confidence I'm talking about is confidence in God. It insulates us from the damaging effects of fear. God wants us to have confidence (faith and trust) that He loves us and is working on our behalf.

Imagine you are a singer and have been given the opportunity to sing a duet at the local talent show. Also, you just happen to have the world's most famous vocalist as your friend and duet partner. Would you panic before you went onstage? Of course not! You would sing with confidence, knowing that your partner's talent would carry you both through. This is how it is with God. He is always with you. There is no need to worry or fear. You can place your confidence in Him.

Today's Thought

When you have a confident assurance that God is on your side—that He is working on your behalf—you can resist fear and enjoy your life.

Dig Deeper into God's Word: Study 2 Corinthians 7:16; Psalm 71:5

Breaking the Habit of Discouragement

But David encouraged and strengthened himself in the Lord his God. (1 Samuel 30:6 AMPC)

One of the great benefits of quiet time with God is that it encourages your soul. The more time you spend studying the Word of God and discovering His promises, the more positive and encouraged you will be.

For many people, discouragement is a habit. It is the way they naturally respond to any challenge or problem. For many years, I had a habit of getting discouraged and feeling sorry for myself when I had problems, but I broke that habit with God's help and have formed the better habit of going to God to receive encouragement and choosing to be joyful whether I get my way or not.

With God's help you can begin to break the habit of discouragement. Choose to react to situations with faith rather than fear, with hope rather than dread. Ask God to help you develop a joyful, trusting, optimistic response no matter what situation you face.

Today's Thought

Life is too precious a gift to waste any of it stuck in discouragement and despair. Think about the good things God has done in your life... and believe for many more things to come.

Dig Deeper into God's Word: Study Joshua 1:9;
   Ephesians 3:13

Thinking about What You Think About

Casting down arguments and every high thing that exalts itself against the knowledge of God, bringing every thought into captivity to the obedience of Christ. (2 Corinthians 10:5 NKJV)

Most people don't pay attention to the thoughts they are thinking. They meditate on whatever thought comes to their mind, regardless of how destructive that thought may be.

I encourage you to determine that with God's help you are going to focus on positive, faith-filled thoughts and cast any negative thoughts aside.

We are in a spiritual war, and the mind is the battlefield. We either win or lose our battles based on winning the war in our minds. If you choose to think according to the Word of God, your emotions will start lining up with your thoughts. If you have had years of experiencing wrong thinking and letting your emotions lead you, making this change will take time and effort... but God will help you each step of the way, and the results will be worth it!

Today's Thought

With God's help, you can choose the thoughts you focus on. Don't say, "I'm just an emotional person, and I can't help the way I think or feel." You can learn to think as God thinks!

Dig Deeper into God's Word: Study Proverbs 12:5; Philippians 3:13–15

Listening for God's Voice

The sheep that are My own hear My voice and listen to Me;
I know them, and they follow Me. (John 10:27)

God wants to communicate with you in a personal way. He wants to lead you to the good things He has in store for you. Talking with God and hearing from Him should be the natural way that we live.

One man was asked how he learned to hear from God and he answered, "By making a lot of mistakes." God often speaks to me by giving me an idea of what I need to do in order to solve a problem that I have. At other times I find that I either have or don't have peace about a direction I am ready to take. He speaks through His Word, and at times He speaks through other people. God will communicate with you in a way that is comfortable and right for you.

I don't always hear perfectly, and neither will you, but I have learned that being guided by God in my daily life is an exciting and powerful way for me to live.

Today's Thought

Spending regular time with God will help you learn to be led by the Spirit of God all day long.

Dig Deeper into God's Word: Study Deuteronomy 5:27;
    Mark 4:23

The Why Question

He will not fear bad news; his heart is steadfast, trusting [confidently relying on and believing] in the Lord. (Psalm 112:7)

When we find ourselves in the midst of a struggle or adversity, we often ask God, "Why? Why is this happening to me?"

Let's imagine, for one moment, that God actually answered that question. Would His explanation change anything? The effects of the situation would still be with you. What would you have learned?

When we ask God that question, what we're really asking is, "God, do You love me? Will You take care of me in my sorrow and pain? You won't leave me alone, will You?" Is it possible that we ask for explanations because we're afraid God doesn't truly care about us?

Instead, we can learn to say, "Lord, I believe. I don't understand, and I'll probably never grasp all the reasons bad things happen, but I know for certain that You love me, You are good, and You are with me—always."

Today's Thought

It takes more faith to go through something victoriously than to be delivered from it. Put your faith in God, and you'll come out stronger on the other side.

Dig Deeper into God's Word: Study Romans 8:28;
    Jeremiah 17:7

Healthy Expectations

And now, Lord, for what do I expectantly wait? My hope
[my confident expectation] is in You. (Psalm 39:7)

It is only natural to have expectations of people and circumstances,
but it should only be from God that we expect the very best. Any
other expectations could just lead us to disappointment and
frustration.

This is why it is important for us to reexamine our expectations,
making sure that our expectations and hope are in God, not in a
person, a job, or a circumstance that could let us down.

I'm not saying that you can never trust people—God often
uses people in our lives. The key is to ask God, in your quiet time,
for what you need and then trust Him to work through whom-
ever He chooses. When God is your source, you'll never end up
disappointed.

Today's Thought

God may not give you exactly what you are expecting, but
He will definitely give you what is best.

Dig Deeper into God's Word: Study Philippians 1:20;
    Romans 8:25

Living with Excellence

*Whatever you do [whatever your task may be], work from
the soul [that is, put in your very best effort], as [something
done] for the Lord and not for men.* (Colossians 3:23)

Whatever God has placed before you to do—whether it is working
in a career, raising a family, being a friend, starting a ministry—He
wants you to do it with excellence. He wants you to do your absolute best for Him.

Mediocrity is easy. Anybody can do it. But it is costly. It costs us
fulfillment. And it costs us real joy. One way to find purpose and
joy in life is to pray in your quiet time with God that He will always
help you to be excellent in all you do each day.

This doesn't mean you will be perfect. We all make mistakes and
stumble from time to time. But with God's help, you can learn from
those mistakes and purpose to do every new thing before you with
excellence in service to Him.

Today's Thought

*It is only when you refuse to settle for mediocrity that
you'll really begin to discover how much you are capable
of doing.*

Dig Deeper into God's Word: Study 2 Corinthians 8:7;
    Colossians 3:1

Great Things to Say

Pleasant words are like a honeycomb, sweet and delightful to the soul and healing to the body. (Proverbs 16:24)

We often focus on the things we *shouldn't* say, but it is just as important (if not more so) to focus on the things we *should* say. Here are a few examples from God's Word of things we can say that will benefit our lives:

- *Bless everything you can possibly bless.* James 3:8–10 says we have the power to bless or curse with the words of our mouth. Choose to use your words to be a blessing.
- *Be thankful and say so.* (See Psalm 100:4.) Don't just think about how much you appreciate someone—tell them! It will make their day—and yours.
- *Be an encourager.* (See Hebrews 10:24–25.) Make an effort to give someone an encouraging word every day. This is a practice that will change the way you view other people and yourself.

In your quiet time with God, ask Him to show you opportunities to bless others, show gratitude, and encourage someone close by.

Today's Thought

It's never too late to change your conversation. Use your words to build up others and yourself. They are powerful tools that God has given you.

Dig Deeper into God's Word: Study Exodus 4:15; John 12:50

Take a Step

Your word is a lamp to my feet and a light to my path.
(Psalm 119:105)

If God has given you a goal or put a dream in your heart, it is important that you take a step toward accomplishing that goal or realizing that dream.

In order to live His abundant, confident, joy-filled life, it's important to understand you have a part to play. Don't sit back in fear and passivity; instead, act in faith and take that bold first step.

Whether it's signing up for a class, making a phone call, recruiting others to help you, writing the first chapter of the book you have wanted to write...whatever it is, take a step of faith.

You may not be sure how it's going to work out. You might not even know what the second step will be. But if you do your part, there is one thing you can know for sure: God promises He will do His part in your life.

Today's Thought

If you focus on God's promises rather than potential problems, you'll quickly see things in your life turn around for the best.

Dig Deeper into God's Word: Study Psalm 26:3;
    Psalm 16:8

Refuse to Quit

Do not grow tired or lose heart in doing good [but continue doing what is right without weakening]. (2 Thessalonians 3:13)

There are times when individuals will come to me for advice and prayer, and when I tell them what the Word of God says or what I think the Holy Spirit is saying, their response is, "I know that's right; God has been showing me the same thing. But, Joyce, it's just too hard."

There were times in my past when I said the same thing to God: *Lord, this is just too hard.* But God graciously showed me that this is a lie the enemy tries to inject into our minds to get us to give up. God's instructions are never too difficult for us to obey.

You can always walk in obedience to God because He has given His Spirit to work powerfully within us to help us at all times (see John 14:16). The Holy Spirit is with us, and He will enable us to do anything and everything God asks of us.

Today's Thought

Anytime God guides you in a particular direction, it is for your benefit. And when you lean on and rely on God's grace, you can accomplish everything He asks you to do.

Dig Deeper into God's Word: Study Hebrews 6:1;
   Job 17:9

Putting Others First

It is more blessed [and brings greater joy] to give than to receive. (Acts 20:35)

One of the very best things you can do to make any day better is to take your focus off of yourself and begin looking for ways to help and serve others. It is a heavenly paradox: The more you help others, the more you are helped. This is why Jesus said that it is more blessed to give than to receive.

Rather than complaining about your problems or your terrible day, take some quiet time with God and contemplate how to solve someone else's problems and brighten their day. Think of them, pray for them, and ask God to give you a fresh idea of how to bless them. Putting others first is a revolutionary new outlook on life that will bring you the peace and joy that only God can give.

Today's Thought

Start doing little things on a regular basis to help family, friends, and even strangers. You'll be surprised at how much fun you'll have in the process!

Dig Deeper into God's Word: Study Philippians 2:3; 1
    Corinthians 10:24

Be Bold and Unafraid to Fail

*For God did not give us a spirit of timidity or cowardice or
fear, but [He has given us a spirit] of power and of love and
of sound judgment and personal discipline [abilities that
result in a calm, well-balanced mind and self-control].* (2
Timothy 1:7)

Throughout Scripture, God calls us to be bold—to be brave, daring, courageous, and valiant.

If you have a tendency to avoid taking chances in life because
you're afraid of making mistakes, God wants you to know He's
pleased when you're at least bold enough to try. It doesn't matter if
you don't do everything exactly right. What does matter is that you
step out in faith, believing God will help you.

God has given us a "spirit of power," and He wants us to use it!
It doesn't take courage to do what we already know we can do. True
courage is displayed when you're afraid to do something but you
go ahead and do it anyway. The truth is, we don't ever have to give
in to fear, because we can ask God for His help anytime we need it.

Today's Thought

*The biggest mistake you can make is to be afraid of making
one.*

Dig Deeper into God's Word: Study Matthew 14:27;
    Ezekiel 22:14

Spending Time with God

Early in the morning, while it was still dark, Jesus got up, left [the house], and went out to a secluded place, and was praying there. (Mark 1:35)

Getting to know God intimately requires regular study of His Word, spending time talking with Him in prayer, and choosing to believe He loves you and has a great plan for you. It's about inviting God into every facet of your life.

There will be days when you don't *feel* like praying, reading the Word, or serving God, and there will be days when you don't necessarily *feel* God's presence.

These are the days when you simply refuse to live controlled by your feelings. Instead, ask God to help you walk in obedience and submit to His Word whether you feel like it or not. I often say that if we truly desire to live victoriously, then *we must be willing to do what is right when it feels wrong.*

Today's Thought

The more time you spend with God, the more prepared you'll be to handle any challenge, obstacle, or opportunity that comes your way.

Dig Deeper into God's Word: Study Colossians 1:23; Psalm 88:13

Don't Let Anyone Stop You

We speak, not as [if we were trying] to please people [to gain power and popularity], but to please God who examines our hearts [expecting our best]. (1 Thessalonians 2:4)

Have you ever noticed that some of the most difficult resistance can come from the people closest to you? Longtime friends, trusted colleagues, and even family members can be the first people to discourage you when you begin to tell them about the decisions you're making for God.

These people aren't necessarily bad, but they can be a bad influence in your life if you allow them to hold you back from God's best. Sadly, if people aren't ready to move forward themselves, they often try to hold us back in order to feel better about their own lack of initiative.

Don't let others keep you from receiving the new things God has for you. Don't let their accusation or rejection determine your decisions. Pray for them, love them, but don't let them hold you back from God's best.

Today's Thought

Whatever you desire today—new health, a new mindset, a new attitude, a new relationship, a new boldness, a new career—remember, it takes perseverance and determination. Keep going forward, no matter what.

Dig Deeper into God's Word: Study Psalm 23:4; Judges 18:6

Place Your Trust in God

Some trust in chariots and some in horses, but we will remember and trust in the name of the Lord our God. (Psalm 20:7)

Where have you placed your trust? Who or what do you depend on to carry you through?

Is your trust in your job, employer, bank account, or friends? Perhaps your trust is in yourself, your past record of successes, education, natural talents, or possessions. These things are all important, but you must realize they are all temporal, subject to change. God is the only One who doesn't change. He alone is the Rock that cannot be moved.

As children of God, we can have the assurance that God will deliver us in current troubles, just as He delivered us in the past. We can take our trust and put it in the right place, which is in God alone.

Trust is not worried or anxious, because it has entered into God's rest. Trust is not confused, because it has no need to lean on its own understanding. Trust does not give up or panic. Trust believes that God is good and that He works all things out for our good.

Today's Thought

Trusting God may not always be easy, but it brings great reward. He is the only source of strength that never fails. You can depend on Him today.

Dig Deeper into God's Word: Study Proverbs 3:5; Psalm 40:4

What Are You Thinking About?

Whatever is true, whatever is honorable and worthy of respect, whatever is right and confirmed by God's word... if there is anything worthy of praise, think continually on these things [center your mind on them, and implant them in your heart]. (Philippians 4:8)

Notice that in the above scripture Paul doesn't say we should just occasionally think about the good things—he says we are to center our minds on them. That means that each and every day, we should take some quiet time with God and begin to think about what we are thinking about. Rather than dwell on all that is going wrong, we can choose to dwell on all that is going right.

What you think about—what you focus on—is going to affect how you see life. If you determine to focus on God's goodness and His promises, which are true, pure, lovely, kind, and gracious, you won't succumb to the pressures of stress. No matter what happens during the course of your day, you'll be able to trust God and enjoy His peace.

Today's Thought

You don't have to be panicked; you can be peaceful. You don't have to be overloaded; you can be overjoyed. That's what happens when you choose to focus on the good things God has done and is doing on your behalf.

Dig Deeper into God's Word: Study Isaiah 55:8–9; 1 Corinthians 2:16

God's Appointed Time

For the vision is yet for the appointed [future] time. It hurries toward the goal [of fulfillment]; it will not fail. Even though it delays, wait [patiently] for it, because it will certainly come; it will not delay. (Habakkuk 2:3)

God rarely seems to be in a hurry about anything, and we are usually in a hurry about *everything*. Our human nature is to be rushed and impatient. We are not satisfied to know that God will make a way; we want to know *when* He will make a way.

Scripture promises us that at the appointed time, God will do what needs to be done, but when is the appointed time? It is the time that God determines is the right time, and He rarely lets us know how long that will be. We can, however, be assured that it won't be longer than we can endure. Our Lord knows what we need, and He knows exactly when we need it. He is never late—He always moves at the exact perfect time.

Today's Thought

God has already been where we are going, and He already knows exactly what will happen.

Dig Deeper into God's Word: Study Psalm 102:13; Acts 17:26

Choosing Peace

Peace I leave with you; My [perfect] peace I give to you; not as the world gives do I give to you. Do not let your heart be troubled, nor let it be afraid. (John 14:27)

The more time you spend with God, the more peace you will have in your life.

A life without peace is a life full of frustration. It is the result of focusing on things you can't do anything about. When you worry about things beyond your control, stress and anxiety begin to creep into your life.

The apostle Paul said, "Be anxious for nothing, but in everything by prayer and supplication, with thanksgiving, let your requests be made known to God; and the peace of God, which passes all understanding, will guard your hearts and minds through Christ Jesus" (Philippians 4:6–7 NKJV).

Once we realize we are struggling with something and feel upset, we can start praying and immediately turn the situation over to God, trusting Him to help us. You and I are not called to a life of frustration and struggle. Jesus came so we could have righteousness, joy, and peace!

Today's Thought

Peace is never dependent on the circumstances around you. With God's help, you can have peace in the midst of any storm. Peace allows you to enjoy life even when life is imperfect.

Dig Deeper into God's Word: Study Isaiah 9:6;
     James 3:18

Expecting God's Best

May the God of hope fill you with all joy and peace in believing [through the experience of your faith] that by the power of the Holy Spirit you will abound in hope and overflow with confidence in His promises. (Romans 15:13)

Hope is one of the most powerful forces in the universe. And as a child of God, you can be filled with hope.

Hope is the happy anticipation that something good is going to happen in your life. It's about expecting the best. What are you expecting? Have you even thought about it? If you're expecting nothing, or if you are expecting just a little bit, you are going to get what you expect.

I always say, "I'd rather believe for a whole lot and get half of it than believe for a little bit and get all of it."

God wants you to place your hope in Him and have a happy expectation for something good. If you're in a tough situation today, expect it to change. If you're in a good situation today, expect it to get even better. God is a God of hope!

Today's Thought

Instead of expecting the worst, make a decision to expect the best. In your quiet time with God let Him fill your heart with hope that He is going to do something incredible for you... and through you.

Dig Deeper into God's Word: Study Romans 8:19;
     Luke 8:40

Kingdom Living

*For those who are living according to the flesh set their minds
on the things of the flesh [which gratify the body], but those
who are living according to the Spirit, [set their minds on]
the things of the Spirit [His will and purpose]. (Romans 8:5)*

The Kingdom of God is made up of paradoxes, things that seem counterintuitive. In other words, society tells us to do one thing in order
to succeed, but the Word of God often instructs us to do the exact
opposite. Here are some examples to think about in your quiet time:

- The world tells us to push our way to the front of the line or
  top of the ladder to be first, but the Bible tells us that the last
  will be first, and the first will be last (see Matthew 20:16).
- The world tells us to be stingy and greedy, but the Word of
  God tells us to give generously (see Luke 6:38).
- The world tells us to hate our enemies and hold grudges, but
  the Word of God tells us to love our enemies and pray for them
  (see Matthew 5:44).
- The world tells us to promote ourselves and to boast about our
  accomplishments to be considered great, but the Bible says that
  the greatest among you will be your servant (see Matthew 23:11).

Live your life in contrast to the selfish ways of the world. God's
instructions will bring the peace and happiness we all desperately need.

Today's Thought

*If you make decisions and act in accordance to God's Word,
your life will be a light in the darkness and a blessing to all
you come in contact with.*

Dig Deeper into God's Word: Study Matthew 6:10;
    Daniel 7:27

Never Give Up!

Let us not become weary in doing good, for at the proper time we will reap a harvest if we do not give up. (Galatians 6:9 NIV)

One of the most important truths you can always hold on to is that God has promised to never leave you—He is always by your side!

No matter how difficult the circumstances may seem around you, don't stop trying. Never give up! God is for you, and He is bigger than any trouble you may be facing.

You can regain anything the devil has stolen from you by leaning on God's grace and not on your own ability. In Galatians 6:9, the apostle Paul simply encourages us to keep on keeping on.

Don't be a quitter. Have an "I can do all things through Christ" attitude. With God's help, you can go all the way through the struggle to complete victory with Him.

Today's Thought

God will give you the strength to face any obstacle before you. Rather than focusing on the problem, believe His promises and boldly keep moving forward.

Dig Deeper into God's Word: Study 2 Chronicles 15:7; 2 Corinthians 4:1

Overcoming Regret and Dread

I sought the Lord [on the authority of His word], and He answered me, and delivered me from all my fears. (Psalm 34:4)

Regret and dread go hand in hand, and they are both rooted in fear. Regrets cause you to fear the consequences of past mistakes, and dreads cause you to fear the consequences of future mishaps. Both assume the worst; neither is from God.

It's a freeing revelation to know that God offers us victory in the midst of difficulty. We are going to make mistakes, but God can redeem them and even use them to educate us for the future.

If you're afraid of your past or afraid of your future, you'll be frozen in a dysfunctional present. There is only one solution, and it comes straight from 1 Peter 5:7: "Casting the whole of your care [all your anxieties, all your worries, all your concerns, once and for all] on Him, for He cares for you" (AMPC). Cast those cares off of your life, and never pick them up again.

Today's Thought

Your mistakes are not greater than God's mercy. All things are possible with God.

Dig Deeper into God's Word: Study Deuteronomy 31:6; 2 Kings 17:39

Take Time to Pray

Be unceasing and persistent in prayer. (1 Thessalonians 5:17)

No matter who you are or what you do—whether you are a mother, a business executive, a mechanic, or a schoolteacher—you are probably busy! But no matter how busy you are, be sure you take time to pray and talk to God. If you do, He will hear you and help you.

Prayer is something you can do throughout the day, no matter how many responsibilities you have. For example, if you are an exhausted stay-at-home mom who cleans up the house and cares for children all day, just take one minute to be still and say, "Oh, Jesus, I love You. Strengthen me right now. God, I need some energy. I am worn-out." Even something that simple is powerful and gets God's attention.

Praying your way through the day allows God to be involved in all aspects of your life. Why struggle when you can have God's presence and help? Your prayer doesn't have to be long or eloquent; it just needs to be sincere.

Today's Thought

"I need You, Lord" is one of the best prayers to pray.

Dig Deeper into God's Word: Study James 5:16;
Job 22:27

Your Feelings Don't Have the Final Say

When I am weak [in human strength], then I am strong [truly able, truly powerful, truly drawing from God's strength].
(2 Corinthians 12:10)

Depending on the day, we may feel happy or sad, excited or discouraged, on top of the mountain or down in the valley, and a thousand other things. Feelings can be very powerful and demanding, but we do not have to live according to how we feel on a particular day.

The truth is that we can learn to manage our emotions rather than allowing them to manage us. This has been one of the most important biblical truths I've learned in my journey with God. It has also been one that has helped me to consistently enjoy my life.

If we have to wait to see how we feel before we know if we can enjoy the day, we are giving our feelings control over us. But thankfully, we have free will, and we can make decisions that are not based on feelings. If we are willing to make right choices regardless of how we feel, God will always be faithful to give us the strength to do so.

Today's Thought

God's Word and His promises for your life are stronger than your feelings. Submit to what God says each day, and your feelings will begin to line up with God's promises.

Dig Deeper into God's Word: Study 2 Samuel 22:33;
    Psalm 68:28

The Other Side of Suffering

And this, so that I may know Him [experientially, becoming more thoroughly acquainted with Him, understanding the remarkable wonders of His Person more completely] and [in that same way experience] the power of His resurrection [which overflows and is active in believers], and [that I may share] the fellowship of His sufferings. (Philippians 3:10)

Nobody wants to go through suffering, but I've discovered there is much we can learn from difficulty. One of the benefits on the other side of suffering is a deeper relationship with God.

When we are put in a position where we have no one who can help us except God and we put our trust in Him, we experience the many wonders of who He is and how good He is. We experience His faithfulness, justice, kindness, mercy, grace, wisdom, and power.

Paul said that his determined purpose was to know Christ and to become more deeply and intimately acquainted with the wonders of His person. He said he wanted to know the power of Christ's resurrection and even share the fellowship of His sufferings. If you are dealing with a difficult situation, go to God in your quiet time and ask Him to use that difficulty to make you into the person He wants you to be.

Today's Thought

Instead of allowing suffering to drive you away from God, use that challenge to help you come closer to Him, trusting and depending on Him more than you ever have before.

Dig Deeper into God's Word: Study Job 11:16;
    Lamentations 3:32

Ask Less, Trust More

For I consider [from the standpoint of faith] that the suf-
ferings of the present life are not worthy to be compared
with the glory that is about to be revealed to us and in us!
(Romans 8:18)

We live life forward, and yet we often can only understand it by
looking back. There are many painful things we do not understand
when they are happening to us. But later, as we look back, we see
things differently than we did before, because we see the good that
has come from the previous pain we endured.

David said, "My heart is not proud, Lord, my eyes are not
haughty; I do not concern myself with great matters or things too
wonderful for me" (Psalm 131:1 NIV).

David was simply saying that there are things hidden in the
mysteries of God that no one can possibly understand. In our quiet
times with God, we would be wise to ask fewer questions and simply trust God more. He will use everything we go through to bring
about His purposes in our lives.

Today's Thought

God sees what you are going through, and He has a plan to
bring you through it stronger, wiser and more blessed than
you were before.

Dig Deeper into God's Word: Study Psalm 31:14;
     Psalm 56:11

Learning to Absolutely Love Your Life

The thief comes only in order to steal and kill and destroy. I came that they may have and enjoy life, and have it in abundance [to the full, till it overflows]. (John 10:10)

Did you know that God wants you to enjoy your life? Well, He does! In fact, part of God's will is for you to enjoy every moment of it. This is something God's Word tells us in many places.

King Solomon, the wisest man who ever lived, said this: "There is nothing better for a man than to eat and drink and assure himself that there is good in his labor. Even this, I have seen, is from the hand of God" (Ecclesiastes 2:24).

Solomon said to make sure we enjoy the good of our labor. That sounds like it is something we must do as an act of our will. This does not mean that all of life becomes a huge party or a vacation, but it does mean that through the power of God we can learn to enjoy the wonderful life Jesus came to give us.

Today's Thought

It's important to be disciplined and to work hard, but it is equally important to enjoy the fruit that work brings. God wants you to have fun and enjoy life—you can do that today!

Dig Deeper into God's Word: Study 1 Peter 3:10; Psalm 119:159

Blessed with Benefits

Bless and affectionately praise the Lord, O my soul, and do not forget any of His benefits. (Psalm 103:2)

You have benefits as a child of God. That's something to get excited about! Other words for benefits are *favors*, *advantages*, and *profits*. That's what you have been given from your Heavenly Father. And in the scripture above, David doesn't say you have only one benefit; he uses the plural *benefits*. That means you have been given many favors and advantages as a child of God.

The benefits aren't something we've earned by impressing God. They are things He freely gives us because we are His children and He loves to bless us. This is why Romans 8:17 says, "And if we are [His] children, then we are [His] heirs also: heirs of God and fellow heirs with Christ [sharing His inheritance with Him]" (AMPC). You've inherited the benefits, the blessings, and the goodness of God. I encourage you to look for God's benefits today and be thankful for each one.

Today's Thought

One of the very best ways you can begin any personal time with God is to thank Him for all of the blessings, advantages, and benefits He has given you.

Dig Deeper into God's Word: Study Psalm 72:17;
    Ephesians 1:3

A New Day with God

*Therefore if anyone is in Christ [that is, grafted in, joined
to Him by faith in Him as Savior], he is a new creature . . .
Behold, new things have come [because spiritual awakening brings a new life]. (2 Corinthians 5:17)*

You are a new creation—that means you don't have to allow the
old things that happened to you to keep affecting your new life
in Christ. You have a new start. You can have your mind renewed
according to the Word of God. Good things are going to happen
to you!

Begin to think positively about your life. God has a perfect plan
for each of us, and it's important for us to think and speak in agreement with His will and plan for us.

In your quiet time with God, always remember that He has
begun a good work in you, and He will bring it to completion (see
Philippians 1:6). So even when you feel discouraged because you
are not making fast progress, always remember that God is working in you and He is making all things new.

Today's Thought

*Even if you don't have any idea what God's will is for you
at this point, you can begin by thinking in faith,* I may not
know God's plan, but I know He loves me. Whatever He
does will be good, and I'll be blessed.

Dig Deeper into God's Word: Study Proverbs 14:22;
Job 42:2

Determination Leads to Victory

I have fought the good and worthy and noble fight, I have finished the race, I have kept the faith [firmly guarding the gospel against error]. (2 Timothy 4:7)

One of the most important traits a Christian can have is determination. A child of God who refuses to give up is one who will enjoy victory. Jesus endured the cross for the joy of the prize awaiting Him (see Hebrews 12:2), and we should do the same thing.

Persistence is necessary, because there will be difficult times in life. Jesus never promised that when we start following Him, we'll no longer deal with problems. Life isn't always easy, but God is always with us. Going through challenges instead of giving up is what makes us strong.

When you feel weary, remember that God is with you and that He is the strength you need to make it through to the finish. Receive His strength now as you wait in His presence.

Today's Thought

If you have big hopes and big dreams for your life, you will need determination to see them come to pass.

Dig Deeper into God's Word: Study Philippians 2:13;
    Psalm 20:6

The Peace of God

I have told you these things, so that in Me you may have [perfect] peace. (John 16:33)

Peace is one of the greatest blessings that God has given us, and when we receive it, peace can be life-changing. Simply desiring a life of peace is not enough. You have to pursue peace with God, peace with yourself, and peace with those around you (see 1 Peter 3:11).

I have found that the more time I spend with God, the more peaceful I am. Quiet times with Him help me focus on what I have instead of what I don't have, allowing me to stay focused on my blessings instead of worrying.

When walking in peace becomes a priority, you will make the effort needed to see it happen. I spent years praying for God to *give* me peace and finally realized He had *already* provided peace, but I had to appropriate it. Jesus said in John 14:27, "Peace I leave with you." Jesus has already provided your peace. Make the decision to walk in that peace today.

Today's Thought

Even though thoughts of worry and fear come to you, you don't have to dwell on them. Instead, you can choose to embrace the peace of God that is already yours in Christ.

Dig Deeper into God's Word: Study 1 Samuel 25:6; Philippians 4:9

Rejoicing No Matter What

Rejoice in the Lord always [delight, take pleasure in Him]; again I will say, rejoice! (Philippians 4:4)

The apostle Paul wrote the verse above while in prison, and the prisons in his day were worse than anything we could imagine. One of the key words in that verse is the word *always*.

Rain or shine, good day or bad, when you're at your highest point or as low as you can go, you can *always* rejoice because God loves you and He is with you. Our joy should not be dependent on what's happening around us, but on the hope we have in Jesus. When we are going through something difficult, we can rejoice that we are going *through* it and that it won't last forever.

Take time each day to simply rejoice. Rejoice that God loves you. Rejoice that He will never leave you. Rejoice that He has a great plan for your life.

Today's Thought

No matter how minor or major the pressure you are facing, it is only part of your journey. It will eventually pass, and things will get better.

Dig Deeper into God's Word: Study 1 Corinthians 13:6; Luke 10:20

Living Selflessly

Do not merely look out for your own personal interests, but also for the interests of others. (Philippians 2:4)

Deciding to help others is more than a good idea; it is one of the biggest secrets to enjoying every day of your life. We cannot be selfish and happy at the same time.

The Bible teaches us that it is more blessed to give than to receive, and I encourage you to embrace this truth: Following the biblical model of putting others ahead of ourselves is one of the best things we can do to enjoy our own lives. Whether it's something small, like helping a friend run an errand, or something bigger, like volunteering a day of each week to serve the less fortunate in your community, it's all important. It's all life-changing!

Today's Thought

When others become your first thought, joy will be your new reality.

Dig Deeper into God's Word: Study 1 Peter 3:8; Luke 6:35

Effortless Prayer

And when you pray, do not use meaningless repetition as
the Gentiles do, for they think they will be heard because
of their many words. (Matthew 6:7)

There are a lot of people who feel their prayers are insufficient
because they compare themselves to others. God is a creative God
and wants each person to have their own individual prayer life.
Your prayer life doesn't have to be just like that of anyone else.

There are certainly proven principles of prayer that you can
follow. For example, Acts 3:1 shows us that the early disciples set
aside certain hours of the day when they would go to a designated
place to pray. That is good self-discipline, but it is not a law or a
rule that we must follow in order to be praying properly.

Have the freedom to establish a prayer schedule that is individually suited to you—and part of that is learning to pray without
ceasing. That means to pray at all times, in all places, with all kinds
of prayer. I like to say, "Pray your way through the day." Let prayer
become like breathing, something you do with ease and without
effort.

Today's Thought

You never have to wait to pray. Each time you see a need
or think of anything you need help with, pray right away!
Prayer is talking to God, and since He is everywhere, we
can talk to Him all the time.

Dig Deeper into God's Word: Study Matthew 6:9;
    Romans 8:26

Celebrating with a Heart of Gratitude

Always giving thanks to God the Father for all things, in the name of our Lord Jesus Christ. (Ephesians 5:20)

All through the Bible, we see people celebrating victory and progress in a variety of ways. One of those ways was to specifically take the time to give an offering to God and to thank Him for His goodness. Noah did it. Abraham did it. And we can do it, too. There are many ways to express gratitude, but the most important thing is that we do it.

Our lives would be a lot happier, and more powerful, if we would take a few moments in our quiet time with God to give thanks for the amazing things He does for us. It is important to be thankful and say so (see Psalm 100:4).

A grateful heart shows a lot about the character of a person. It keeps God first, knowing that He is the source of every blessing we receive. Gratitude wipes away every feeling of entitlement—it's an attitude that says, *I know I don't deserve God's goodness, but I am surely grateful for it.*

Today's Thought

Take time to meditate on the goodness and mercy of God in your life. You can always find ways God has blessed you if you stop and take the time to look.

Dig Deeper into God's Word: Study Psalm 68:3; Psalm 149:2

Laughter Is Good Medicine

*A happy heart is good medicine and a joyful mind causes heal-
ing, but a broken spirit dries up the bones. (Proverbs 17:22)*

Although we all experience difficulty and sadness at times in our
lives, it is important to also find ways to smile and even laugh.
Laughter is good medicine. It has been scientifically proven to
improve health and healing.

No matter what I am going through, it never fails to make me
feel better if I have a good laugh about something, and I think you
will find the same to be true for you.

I think God has given us the ability to laugh for a reason. Of
course, one of the reasons is because He wants us to enjoy life, but I
also believe it has the ability to rescue us from letting our problems
overwhelm us.

Laughter also decreases stress, so why not purposely find something to laugh about today?

Today's Thought

*Take moments throughout the day to relax and laugh a lit-
tle, even if it means laughing at your own mistakes.*

Dig Deeper into God's Word: Study Job 5:22;
Ecclesiastes 3:4

Starting Small

His master said to him, "Well done, good and faithful ser-
vant. You have been faithful and trustworthy over a little,
I will put you in charge of many things; share in the joy of
your master." (Matthew 25:23)

Great victories usually have small beginnings. But there is much to
be said for those small beginnings. For example:

- You may want to have a ministry that reaches the world, but
  God will ask you to *start small*—volunteer at your church and
  be willing to do whatever needs to be done.
- You may be praying that God will give you your own business,
  but God will direct you to *start small*—show up for work on
  time and be faithful at the job you have now.
- You may be trying to figure out how to lose a certain amount
  of weight, but wisdom says to *start small*—cut out sugar-filled
  drinks and exercise for twenty minutes today.

We have a tendency to get so wrapped up in the destination that
we never even begin the journey. What is God asking you to do
today? Whatever it is, be willing to start small and be diligent.

Today's Thought

If you are faithful and take small steps day after day, one
day you'll look back and be amazed at how far you have
traveled.

Dig Deeper into God's Word: Study Psalm 115:13;
    Luke 19:17

Active Faith

But someone may say, "You [claim to] have faith and I have [good] works; show me your [alleged] faith without the works [if you can], and I will show you my faith by my works [that is, by what I do]." (James 2:18)

Faith is always active. It is not a passive endeavor. Faith requires that you believe God's promises and move forward obediently to do what God is telling you to do.

Sometimes we think, *I'm not sure what God is saying to me. I'm afraid I'm going to take the wrong step.* I understand this concern, but did you spot a certain word in there? *Afraid.* When you believe God is giving you a direction to take, don't let fear rule you. Being frozen in fear is never the will of God.

Don't be afraid to take a step because you are afraid it will be the wrong one. God sees your heart. He knows you are trying to please Him and live in obedience to His Word. He is not a cruel, angry God who is going to punish you if you take a misstep along the way. He is faithful to guide you, and even if you take the wrong step, He'll get you back on the right path.

Today's Thought

Be bold and follow God!

Dig Deeper into God's Word: Study Hebrews 11:3;
    Matthew 21:21

Accepted by God

*All that My Father gives Me will come to Me; and the one
who comes to Me I will most certainly not cast out [I will
never, never reject anyone who follows Me]. (John 6:37)*

Have you ever felt rejected, unwanted, or out of place? If so, you're
not alone. There is no one who experiences acceptance from everyone in their life. In fact, some people experience a type of rejection
that damages their souls. We may believe we are flawed if people
have rejected us, and therefore, we mistakenly assume we are
worthless or unlovable.

But this is not true. The truth is that God created you, and He
delights in you. God loves you unconditionally, and He will never
reject you. Don't allow someone else's behavior, words, or actions
toward you to make you feel inferior or unloved.

You can live beyond your feelings—you can move past the pain
of any rejection you may have dealt with in your past. You are
loved, accepted, and approved by your Heavenly Father. His love is
what matters the most.

Today's Thought

*God's thoughts toward you, and His approval of you, are
far more important than what others say or feel. Don't let
the rejection of a person outweigh the approval of God.*

Dig Deeper into God's Word: Study Psalm 6:9;
    Hebrews 13:5

The Strength of His Might

For the Lord your God is He who goes with you, to fight for
you against your enemies, to save you. (Deuteronomy 20:4)

Too many times we try to fight battles in our own strength, and
then, when we inevitably fail, we get frustrated and want to give up.

I suggest that anytime you recognize a challenge ahead of you,
take it to God. In your quiet time with Him, simply pray: *Father,*
I'm feeling worried about the task before me. If it is something You don't
want me to do, please show me, and if You want me to do it, then grant
me grace to do it with joy.

Anytime we take our problems to God and trust Him to fight our
battles for us, we are going to have the ultimate victory. God can do
things through us that we could never do on our own, so don't try
to fight on your own. If you focus on the fact that God is with you
and trust Him in every situation, there is no way you can lose.

Today's Thought

God has never lost a battle; He is undefeated. It would be
foolish to try to handle your problems on your own. Take
them to God and watch Him bring about a victory.

Dig Deeper into God's Word: Study Psalm 66:5–7;
    Colossians 1:11

For the Joy of Obtaining the Prize

Jesus...for the joy [of accomplishing the goal] set before Him endured the cross, disregarding the shame, and sat down at the right hand of the throne of God [revealing His deity, His authority, and the completion of His work]. (Hebrews 12:2)

Jesus said that even though He despised the shame of the cross, He endured it for the joy of obtaining the prize on the other side of it. Numerous people have told me that they wouldn't trade what they went through for anything, simply because of how it changed them and brought them closer to God.

We may despise what we are going through while we are going through it. No one enjoys any kind of pain or suffering. But if we can believe that something good will come from the pain, we will be able to endure it more joyfully. If we continue having faith that we will see the goodness of God no matter how bad we hurt or how long it takes, we will taste the sweetness of breakthrough and victory.

Today's Thought

You have to go through to get through. Don't be afraid of difficulty, because God will not give you more than you can handle with Him in your life, helping and guiding you.

Dig Deeper into God's Word: Study 1 Corinthians 9:24; 1 Thessalonians 5:9

The Importance of Waiting Well

And let endurance have its perfect result and do a thorough work, so that you may be perfect and completely developed [in your faith], lacking in nothing. (James 1:4)

We all have to wait for things in life. This is why patience is extremely important if you want to enjoy your life and glorify God with your behavior.

The next time you have to wait on something or someone, instead of reacting impatiently, try reminding yourself, *Getting upset will not make this go any faster, so I might as well enjoy the wait.* You can even say out loud, "I am developing patience as I wait, so I am thankful in this situation." If you do that, you will be acting on the Word of God rather than reacting to the unpleasant circumstance.

Remember, patience is a fruit of the Spirit that God wants to develop in your life. Don't merely think about how hard and frustrating it is, but think about how blessed you can be as you learn the art of waiting well.

Today's Thought

We will all experience seasons of waiting at different times in our lives, so we might as well discover joy in those times and lean on God while we wait for the answer.

Dig Deeper into God's Word: Study Genesis 49:18; Lamentations 3:25–26

A Letter for You

Your word is a lamp to my feet and a light to my path.
(Psalm 119:105)

The Bible is written as a personal letter to you from God. He speaks to you, meets your needs, and guides your steps through His written Word. He reveals truth and wisdom and teaches you how to live.

There is an answer for every problem in the Word of God. There may be times when God speaks something to your heart that is not specifically stated in a chapter and verse of the Bible, but it will always be in agreement with the principles in His Word.

Without spending time in God's Word, we can't hear His voice clearly and accurately. Knowing the written Word protects us from deception—it's our standard of truth. Listening for God's voice without being consistently in His Word opens you up to hearing voices, or being influenced by sources, that are not from God, which is why it's so important to not only read His Word, but to study it. Make Bible study a top priority, because it is your instruction book for life!

Today's Thought

God's Word is His gift to you, giving you direction and shining a light on your steps. Take time today to read some of God's personal letter to you, and ask Him to speak to your heart.

Dig Deeper into God's Word: Study Psalm 1:1-2;
   Galatians 5:16

See the Good and
Believe the Best

*Love bears all things [regardless of what comes], believes
all things [looking for the best in each one], hopes all things
[remaining steadfast during difficult times], endures all
things [without weakening]. (1 Corinthians 13:7)*

The Bible teaches us to always see the good in people and believe
the best of every person.

But if we let our thoughts lead our lives, they usually tend toward
negativity. Our flesh, without the influence of the Holy Spirit, is
dark and negative. Thankfully, we don't have to walk in the flesh,
but we can choose to be led by the Spirit (see Romans 8:5). When
we choose to let the Spirit lead us, we will see the best in other
people, and we will be filled with God's love and peace in our souls.

In your time with God, ask Him to help you see other people as
His children rather than as adversaries. Decide to look past their
faults and see them as God sees them. Allow the Holy Spirit to help
you see the best in every person in your life.

Today's Thought

*God has forgiven your sins; He doesn't hold them against
you. Ask Him to help you do the same with the other people
in your life.*

Dig Deeper into God's Word: Study Mark 12:31;
    James 2:8

Remembering God's Goodness

Bless and affectionately praise the Lord, O my soul, and all that is [deep] within me, bless His holy name. (Psalm 103:1)

One of the things I love about the Bible is how practical it is for daily living. Psalm 103 encourages us to remember the blessings of God in our lives, and then gives us a list of His goodness. Here are a few of the things you can thank God for in your time with Him today:

- Your sins are forgiven (v. 3).
- Healing is yours (v. 3).
- God redeems your life (v. 4).
- You've been made beautiful, dignified, and noble (v. 4).
- God loves you unconditionally (vv. 4 and 11–12).
- God cares for you and provides for you (v. 5).
- You're strong, overcoming, and soaring (v. 5).
- God is your defender (v. 6).
- When you mess up, God will forgive you (vv. 10–12).
- God knows you better than you know yourself (v. 14).
- No matter what happens, God will never stop loving you (v. 17).

What an amazing list! I encourage you to study Psalm 103 today and thank God for His great love for you.

Today's Thought

God loves you so much that He has poured out His blessings, benefits, and goodness on your life. Don't get so accustomed to His love that you take it for granted. Thank Him each day for His blessings in your life.

Dig Deeper into God's Word: Study Lamentations 3:22–26; Psalm 23:5–6

Jesus Understands

For we do not have a High Priest who is unable to sympa-thize and understand our weaknesses and temptations, but One who has been tempted [knowing exactly how it feels to be human] in every respect as we are, yet without [commit-ting any] sin. (Hebrews 4:15)

We can turn to Jesus in our difficulty because He is a High Priest who understands our weaknesses and infirmities. How can He understand? He understands because He has been tempted in all points just as we are, and yet He never sinned. Also, He felt all of our pain and carried all of our burdens when He was on the cross. He knows what you're going through.

You are never alone. Jesus is acquainted with sickness and grief, pain and rejection. You can always turn to Jesus when you are hurt-ing. He is compassionate and understanding. He will never turn you away. Instead, He will listen to your prayer and comfort you in your pain. And best of all, He will carry you through and bring you to the other side stronger than ever before.

Today's Thought

Don't believe the lie of the enemy that you are all alone and no one understands what you are going through. Jesus understands, and He has promised to never leave you or forsake you.

Dig Deeper into God's Word: Study Matthew 26:38; Hebrews 2:17–18

Grace for Daily Living

Therefore as you have received Christ Jesus the Lord, walk in [union with] Him [reflecting His character in the things you do and say—living lives that lead others away from sin]. (Colossians 2:6)

We may know and understand that by God's grace, our sins have been forgiven, but we don't always understand that we need the same grace for daily living that we needed for our salvation.

Many times, living the Christian life seems like it takes a lot of work and effort, and no matter how hard we try, we feel like we are failing. We get frustrated because we want to be what God's Word instructs us to be, but we feel like we don't have the power to behave accordingly.

But God's Word teaches us to live for Jesus in the same way that we received Him—by grace. We are saved by grace, and we are to live by grace. When we do, we'll have the peace and joy of the Holy Spirit, and we'll live the powerful lives God has called us to live.

Today's Thought

Grace is God's underserved favor, and it is the power and ability needed for you to do whatever God asks you to do. His grace saves you, and then it carries you successfully through your journey with Him.

Dig Deeper into God's Word: Study John 1:14;
    James 4:6

The Key to Loving Others

This is the second: You shall [unselfishly] love your neigh-
bor as yourself. There is no other commandment greater
than these. (Mark 12:31)

It's nearly impossible to love others when you don't love the person
God has created you to be. People who haven't learned to accept
that they're imperfect and that God's work in their lives is a process tend to have more difficulty accepting and getting along with
others.

When you learn to love yourself as God's creation in a wholesome and balanced way, you can be patient with yourself as God
changes you. Doing so will also help you be patient with others,
and your relationships will improve. The better you feel about
yourself, the better you'll feel about others. Remember, you can't
give something away if you haven't first received it. God loves and
accepts you, so receive it by faith and then give that same love and
acceptance to others.

Today's Thought

The Bible says that you have been fearfully and wonder-
fully made. God took special care when He created you. So
don't put yourself down or doubt your worth. He loves you,
so you can love yourself, too—imperfections and all.

Dig Deeper into God's Word: Study 1 Peter 1:22;
    Romans 13:9

The Source of Your Confidence

*For You are my hope; O Lord God, You are my trust and the
source of my confidence from my youth. (Psalm 71:5)*

When you put your trust in God, you are able to enter His rest, and
rest is a place of peace where we are able to enjoy our lives while
being confident God is truly for us.

God cares for us; He promises to meet our needs, so we can stop
thinking and worrying about them. I realize this is easier said than
done, but there is no time like the present to begin learning a new
way to live—a way of living that is without worry, anxiety, or fear.

This is the time to begin believing and saying, *God, I trust You
completely. I have no need to worry or be afraid! I will not give in to
fear or anxiety any longer. You are the source of my confidence.* The
more you think about this truth, the more you will find yourself
choosing trust over worry and faith over fear.

Today's Thought

Replace worry with trusting God and enjoy your life.

Dig Deeper into God's Word: Study Job 4:6;
Proverbs 3:26

The Beauty of Righteousness

But to the one who does not work [that is, the one who does not try to earn his salvation by doing good], but believes and completely trusts in Him who justifies the ungodly, his faith is credited to him as righteousness (right standing with God). (Romans 4:5)

Righteousness is given as a free gift to those who sincerely believe in Jesus. You don't have to earn it; you simply receive it.

When we try to be righteous (right before God) through our own effort, it causes struggle and frustration, and it can never truly be attained. Receiving righteousness by faith in Christ allows you to rest in God and appreciate His love and mercy.

For years, I tried so hard to keep the religious rules I thought I had to follow so I could earn righteousness, but this just caused me frustration and agony. I was trying to get to God through good behavior, yet I always fell short.

Jesus invites all of us who are striving for works-based righteousness to give it up and receive God's righteousness by putting our faith in Him. This is a better way to live, and when we choose to receive His righteousness, then His peace, rest, and joy are the natural by-products of our lives.

Today's Thought

The righteousness of God is not earned, but received by placing faith in Jesus.

Dig Deeper into God's Word: Study Psalm 119:142;
    Isaiah 32:17

Where Is Your Focus?

Looking unto Jesus, the author and finisher of our faith.
(Hebrews 12:2 NKJV)

What we focus on will determine the direction of our lives. This is why the Word of God instructs us to look away from all that distracts us and to focus on Jesus, who is the author and finisher of our faith.

The person or thing we focus on becomes magnified in our minds. If we focus on our problems, we continually roll them over and over in our minds, which is like meditating on them. The more we think and talk about our problems, the larger they become. A relatively insignificant distraction can grow into a huge issue merely because we're focusing on it.

In your quiet time with God, meditate on God's Word and His promises rather than the problems you may be facing. When you do, you will see the faithfulness of God revealed, and your problems won't seem so big after all.

Today's Thought

Refuse to rehearse the challenges, distractions, or problems you may be facing. Instead, think and talk about God and His goodness for your life.

Dig Deeper into God's Word: Study 2 Corinthians 4:18; Matthew 6:33

Continually Content

Not that I speak from [any personal] need, for I have learned to be content [and self-sufficient through Christ, satisfied to the point where I am not disturbed or uneasy] regardless of my circumstances. (Philippians 4:11)

One of our goals as Christians should be to say with the apostle Paul, "I have learned to be content . . . regardless of my circumstances."

Paul goes on to say that he had learned how to be satisfied to the point where he was not disturbed whether he had abundance or was in need (see Philippians 4:12). That is the picture of godly contentment!

Being content does not mean that we never want to see any change or that we have no vision for better things, but it does mean that we are not allowing the things we want and don't have yet to steal the enjoyment of what we have at the present time. The more time we spend with God, focusing on His goodness and thanking Him for His promises, the more content we will be with all that He has done—*and is going to do*—in our lives.

Today's Thought

One of the most important things you can learn to do is to enjoy where you are on the way to where you are going.

Dig Deeper into God's Word: Study 1 Timothy 6:6–8

Satisfied Not to Know

For I determined not to know anything among you except Jesus Christ and Him crucified. (1 Corinthians 2:2 NKJV)

If we have no unanswered questions in our lives, then there is no need for faith. We might say that faith often takes the place of answers. If we are wise, we will seek to know the Word, to know God, and to know His will instead of endlessly seeking to know all the answers regarding our everyday circumstances.

When people ask what we are going to do when we encounter a problem, we can simply say, "I don't know yet." Tell people you are praying about everything and that you are assured in your heart that God will give you direction at just the right time. You may not have all the answers, but never forget: You have a close, personal relationship with the One who does!

Today's Thought

There are some things in our walk with God that can be understood only with the heart, not the mind.

Dig Deeper Into God's Word· Study 1 Corinthians 8:2; Philippians 3:8

Let Prayer Lead the Way

*A man's mind plans his way [as he journeys through life],
but the Lord directs his steps and establishes them. (Proverbs 16:9)*

Many times, we make our plans according to what we want to see
take place, instead of even considering what God might want. This
is why the most basic step of faith we can take regarding our situation in life is saying, "Lord, this is what I would like to see happen,
but may Your will be done and not mine!"

Prayer should precede every important decision that we make—
this is another reason why daily time with the Lord is so important. Our presumptions and assumptions can lead us in the wrong
direction. Don't make the mistake of planning and then praying
that God will make your plans work. Pray first and let the Holy
Spirit guide you into God's great plan for your life.

Today's Thought

*The plan you have in mind for your life may look good, but
the plan God has for you is better than you can imagine.
You'll never be sorry when you seek His plan, His purpose,
and His will for your life.*

Dig Deeper into God's Word: Study Matthew 18:19;
     Psalm 102:17

Determined to Overcome

For the Lord God helps Me... Therefore, I have made My
face like flint, and I know that I shall not be put to shame.
(Isaiah 50:7)

Jesus is with you, and because He is with you, you are not going to
be defeated. It's important to always remember that no matter what
you face, you can overcome it. That doesn't mean that things will
always be easy, but if you are determined to keep moving forward,
you *will* make progress with God's help.

In your quiet time with the Lord, thank Him that you are more
than a conqueror in Christ Jesus (see Romans 8:37). In every area
of your life, the only way you can lose is if you give up. So choose to
be determined, even in the toughest circumstances.

God is with you (see Joshua 1:9), and He has promised to never
leave your side (see Matthew 28:20). Hold on to those promises so
that you can live a confident, determined, never-give-up life.

Today's Thought

Sometimes the most important step you can take is sim-
ply the next step. Be determined to keep moving forward
today. Don't let anything cause you to quit or turn back.

Dig Deeper into God's Word: Study Proverbs 16:3; 1
    Samuel 12:22

What's Different about Today?

And He has filled him with the Spirit of God, with wisdom and skill, with intelligence and understanding, and with knowledge in all [areas of] craftsmanship, to devise artistic designs. (Exodus 35:31–32)

God is amazingly creative, and His Spirit dwells in you. You were created in His image, so that means you, too, are creative.

Have you ever been hesitant or afraid to try anything new? Do you ever feel stuck in a rut because your days are filled with the same unenergetic routine? Well, there is something you need to realize about yourself: A great deal of creativity lies within you, and God wants to show you how to tap into that creativity.

I think God enjoys variety—why else would He have put so much of it in us? The old expression is true: Variety is the spice of life.

As you pray about the day ahead of you, ask God what you can do that is new or different. Sometimes even a slight deviation from sameness is refreshing. Always walk in wisdom, but don't be afraid to step out and try something new. God has filled you with creativity and originality—be bold and do something you have never done before.

Today's Thought

Every new day is a brand-new opportunity. Look for something exciting, fun, and new to do today to enjoy the life God has given you.

Dig Deeper into God's Word: Study Joshua 1:8; Psalm 27:4

Good Things Are on the Way

The Lord is good to those who wait [confidently] for Him,
to those who seek Him [on the authority of God's word].
(Lamentations 3:25)

Sometimes when you've had a long series of painful or disappointing things happen, you can get to a point where you are just expecting more of what you've already had. But if you are expecting something bad to happen, those expectations will steal your joy and make it almost impossible to live a victorious life.

Instead of expecting the worst, choose to expect the best. Decide in your quiet time with God that you are going to hope for and expect good things. When you do, this opens the door to God's plan in your life (see Lamentations 3:25).

The next time you are having a bad day, examine your expectations, and if you find they are not what they should be, you can quickly make an adjustment that will bring God's reassuring peace and uncontainable joy back into your life.

Today's Thought

The things that have happened to you in the past are not
what define your future. God's Word defines your future,
and He promises that good things are on the horizon (see
Jeremiah 29:11).

Dig Deeper into God's Word: Study Psalm 103:5;
   Psalm 107:9

Set a Goal

*I press on toward the goal to win the [heavenly] prize of the
upward call of God in Christ Jesus. (Philippians 3:14)*

Setting daily goals helps you see certain dreams come true. That's
because dreams are realized one step at a time, one decision at a
time, one goal at a time.

Goals are essential if you want to be successful in life. It is pointless and even frustrating to have a big dream for your future, or
even a small plan for the day, without setting goals on how you
expect to see those things come true.

When you have a goal and move with a purpose, good things
will happen for you. You may not know how everything is going to
work out. You may not have all the answers for the day ahead. But
if you set a goal (or two, or three), you'll be amazed at how helpful it
can be in improving your outlook for the day ahead.

Today's Thought

*Whether you're a stay-at-home parent, a full-time employee,
a student, a business owner, or a volunteer, goal setting can
help you feel more enthusiastic and joyful about your day
ahead.*

Dig Deeper into God's Word: Study 1 Peter 1:8–9;
    Philippians 3:12

Completely Forgiven

Bless and affectionately praise the Lord, O my soul, and do not forget any of His benefits; who forgives all your sins, who heals all your diseases. (Psalm 103:2–3)

In order to defeat guilt and shame, it is essential that we remember we are forgiven. We can stop thinking about our past failures and begin to praise God, thanking Him for His perfect forgiveness in our lives.

Here are a few scriptures to meditate on in your quiet time with God:

- "As far as the east is from the west, so far has He removed our transgressions from us" (Psalm 103:12).
- "Therefore there is now no condemnation [no guilty verdict, no punishment] for those who are in Christ Jesus [who believe in Him as personal Lord and Savior]" (Romans 8:1).
- "If we [freely] admit that we have sinned and confess our sins, He is faithful and just [true to His own nature and promises], and will forgive our sins and cleanse us continually from all unrighteousness" (1 John 1:9).

Studying scriptures like these will help you understand who you are in Christ and embrace the great future God has in store for your life.

Today's Thought

No matter what you may have done in the past, learn to receive God's forgiveness and see yourself as a new creation in Christ Jesus who is completely forgiven.

Dig Deeper into God's Word: Study 2 Corinthians 2:10; Luke 5:20

Real Giving Costs Something

Remember the words of the Lord Jesus, that He Himself said, "It is more blessed [and brings greater joy] to give than to receive." (Acts 20:35)

Real generosity requires a measure of sacrifice. God gave His only Son to free us, and while we can never equal that sacrifice, when we give of ourselves to others, it is important that we are willing to do so sacrificially.

Giving away the clothes and household items we're finished with may be a nice gesture, but it doesn't equal real giving. Real giving occurs when we give somebody something that we want to keep or that truly costs us something.

When you consider how God gave His only Son for us because of His great love for you, it will compel you to want to give of yourself, too—no matter how much it requires.

Today's Thought

King David said he would not give God something that cost him nothing (see 2 Samuel 24:24).

Dig Deeper into God's Word: Study Psalm 37:21;
    Romans 12:6–8

The Right Kind of Thoughts

For as he thinks in his heart, so is he. (Proverbs 23:7)

The thoughts we allow ourselves to dwell on will set the direction for our lives. This is why I often say, *Where the mind goes, the man follows.*

If we have a negative mind, we will have a negative life. On the other hand, if we renew our mind according to God's Word, we will experience the "good and acceptable and perfect" will of God for our lives (Romans 12:2).

Our struggles and our triumphs are rooted in thinking patterns. Negative thoughts produce discouragement, doubt, and fear, but we don't have to live captive to those thoughts. We can choose to line our thoughts up with the Word of God.

The mind is a battlefield. Ask God to give you the strength to help you start winning the battle today. Decide to resist negative thinking and dwell on positive, faith-filled, godly thoughts for your life instead.

Today's Thought

The more you change your mind for the better, the more your life will also change for the better.

Dig Deeper into God's Word: Study 2 Corinthians 10:5; Colossians 3:2

The Joy of Slowing Down

And the peace of God [that peace which reassures the heart, that peace] which transcends all understanding, [that peace which] stands guard over your hearts and your minds in Christ Jesus [is yours]. (Philippians 4:7)

For so many people, the pace of life is way too fast. They're running from event to event, activity to activity, without ever slowing down to enjoy life. Much of this activity is fueled by a fear that they will miss out on something, and anything that is fueled by fear is unhealthy and spiritually dangerous.

If you find that you're having a hard time finding peace in the midst of all the daily decisions you need to make, I encourage you to slow down. A quiet time with God will help you do that. When you take some time to spend with God, it will help you prioritize all the other events of the day. That time in prayer and study of the Word will give you the right perspective so that you can slow down and draw strength from God to face the decisions and activities of the day in peace.

Today's Thought

Jesus was always busy, but He was never rushed. He wasn't running around, stressing out at the thought of all the things that had to be done. Look to Jesus as your example today.

Dig Deeper into God's Word: Study Isaiah 14:7;
     Matthew 11:28–29

Words Make a Difference

*Pleasant words are as a honeycomb, sweet to the mind and
healing to the body. (Proverbs 16:24 AMPC)*

The Word of God has much to say about the words we choose to
speak. Our words do more than affect the people we are talking to;
our words affect us, too. Your attitudes, emotional stability, peace,
joy—these are all impacted by your own words.

Here are a few biblical directions and encouragements to help
you with your word choices:

- "Do not let unwholesome...words ever come out of your
  mouth, but only such speech as is good for building up others, according to the need and the occasion, so that it will be a
  blessing to those who hear [you speak]" (Ephesians 4:29).
- "But I tell you, on the day of judgment people will have to give
  an accounting for every careless or useless word they speak"
  (Matthew 12:36).
- "Let the words of my mouth and the meditation of my heart
  be acceptable and pleasing in Your sight, O Lord, my [firm,
  immovable] rock and my Redeemer" (Psalm 19:14).

These are just a few of the many encouragements in the Bible
that you can begin to implement in your life. Don't hesitate; you
can start speaking positive words today!

Today's Thought

*Positive, God-inspired words are "sweet to the mind" and
bring "healing to the body."*

Dig Deeper into God's Word: Study Proverbs 12:17;
        Exodus 4:12

Receiving God's Love for You

God's love has been abundantly poured out within our hearts through the Holy Spirit who was given to us. (Romans 5:5)

The Bible teaches us that the love of God has been poured out in our hearts by the Holy Spirit. This simply means that when we accept Jesus as our Savior, He comes to dwell in our hearts in the person of the Holy Spirit...and He brings love with Him, because God is love (see 1 John 4:8).

It's important to ask what we are doing with the love of God that has been freely given to us. Are we receiving His love by faith, believing that He is greater than our failures and weaknesses? Or are we rejecting that love because we've believed the lie of the enemy that we are unlovable?

Take a moment in your quiet time with God to receive His love. When you do that, you will also learn to love yourself—not in a selfish, self-centered way, but in a balanced, godly way, a way that affirms you are God's creation and you are unconditionally loved by your Heavenly Father.

Today's Thought

God's plan is for us to receive His love, to love ourselves in a godly way, to generously love Him in return, and then to love all the people who come into our lives.

Dig Deeper into God's Word: Study Ephesians 3:17–18; 1 John 4:9

The Source of True Joy

You have turned my mourning into dancing for me; You have taken off my sackcloth and clothed me with joy. (Psalm 30:11)

It brings incredible joy when you embrace the truth that you are a forgiven and adored child of God. So why are so many Christians sad, frustrated, and miserable?

I believe it is because they do not understand the reality of being a child of God and the inheritance that is ours in Him. An obstacle or difficulty distracts them, and they simply forget the promises of God for their lives. This is the quickest way to live a sad life instead of a *glad* life.

Jesus did not die to give you a discouraged, defeated, "down" life—He is your glory and lifter of your head (see Psalm 3:3). God has given you everything you need to enjoy Him, to enjoy yourself and the life He has given you. So, look up today. Celebrate His goodness and His blessings in your life. You are a child of the King...let that fill your heart with joy!

Today's Thought

Joy is independent of your circumstances. True joy is found in knowing Christ and the hope that He offers us. Take hold of His promises and walk in gladness, regardless of the circumstances around you.

Dig Deeper into God's Word: Study 1 Thessalonians 2:20; Isaiah 29:19

God Is Trustworthy

When I am afraid, I will put my trust and faith in You.
(Psalm 56:3)

One of the most beautiful things about your life in God is that you can trust Him. Trusting God is an amazing benefit. But it's something we decide to do by faith, not something we necessarily feel.

Trust is what makes a relationship safe and reliable. Think about it this way: We put our money in a bank because it has a good reputation and we decide to trust the institution to keep our money safe. God has a much better reputation than even the best bank in the world, so we can surely decide to deposit our lives with Him and put our total trust in Him.

You can trust God to understand whatever you may be going through because He understands you better than you understand yourself. You can trust Him to help you through any storm, to never reject you, to always be there for you, to be on your side, and to love you unconditionally. He is trustworthy, and He will never let you down!

Today's Thought

Others may have violated your trust, but God never will. Open your heart to Him and choose to put your trust in Him and His great love for you. The more you trust Him, the better your life will be.

Dig Deeper into God's Word: Study Psalm 119:138;
    Psalm 33:4

The Humble Get the Help

Therefore humble yourselves under the mighty hand of God... casting all your cares [all your anxieties, all your worries, and all your concerns, once and for all] on Him, for He cares about you [with deepest affection, and watches over you very carefully]. (1 Peter 5:6–7)

What a powerful scripture! God doesn't just invite us to give our cares to Him—He *instructs* us to. With that in mind, why would we hold on to our worries, our problems, and our cares? The surest way to find joy in our lives is to follow God's guidelines, and they require us to quit worrying.

The cure for worry is humbling ourselves before God in the realization that we are simply not capable of solving all our own problems, and then casting our cares on Him and trusting Him.

Instead of making ourselves miserable, trying to figure everything out on our own, God says we can place our confidence in Him. When we do this we can enter into His rest, totally abandoning ourselves to His care. The promises of God are always obtained by faith and patience.

Today's Thought

It can be scary to let go of things because of concern that God won't act in time, but God is never late... He is always right on time!

Dig Deeper into God's Word: Study Proverbs 29:23; Matthew 5:5

Making a List of Your Blessings

O give thanks to the Lord, for He is good; for His compassion and lovingkindness endure forever! (Psalm 107:1)

Each moment we're given is a precious gift from God. We can choose to have a grateful attitude and live each moment full of joy, simply because God is good and He has given us so much to be thankful for. Here is a short list of things you can thank God for today:

- Your family
- A roof over your head
- The friendships in your life
- The trials God has brought you through
- Clean water
- Your gifts and talents
- The Word of God
- God's unconditional love for you

This list is just a start. Add to this list as you go through the day, thanking God for each and every blessing in your life.

Today's Thought

There is no downside to gratitude. It's one of the healthiest, most joy-filled attitudes you can have. So what are you waiting for? The best time to be thankful is always right now.

Dig Deeper into God's Word: Study 1 Thessalonians 5:18; Psalm 1:1–3

God Chose You

He chose us in Christ [actually selected us for Himself as His own] before the foundation of the world. (Ephesians 1:4)

Let me remind you of something today: You are no surprise to God. He knew what He was getting when He chose you...and He chose you anyway!

The Bible says that God actually *selected us for Himself as His own*. It's no accident that you are a child of God. And He doesn't just put up with you or merely tolerate you. He gladly chose you because He loves you!

God already knew your weaknesses, every flaw you would have, every time you would fail, and He still said, "I want you." Ephesians 1:5 declares that you are adopted as His own. God is your perfect, loving Daddy! With Him on your side, you can be assured things will work out well in the end.

Today's Thought

You can't bother God; you can't impose on Him. He's not frustrated with you when you have a problem. Instead, He'll always meet you with open arms, ready to remind you of how far you have come, how precious you are in His sight, and how much He loves you.

Dig Deeper into God's Word: Study Deuteronomy
    10:15; Mark 13:20

Loving Difficult People

If possible, as far as it depends on you, live at peace with everyone. (Romans 12:18)

Some people are harder than others to love. The truth is that some people are rude or unkind because of the stress they feel or the pain they've experienced in their life. So how do you react to people who are difficult or unkind? Do you respond in love as the Word says we should, or do you stoop to their level, behaving as badly as they do?

As Christians, we have the Word of God and the Holy Spirit in our lives to help us and comfort us, but we must remember that a lot of people in the world who are difficult to get along with don't have that. Jesus said that we have done nothing special if we treat people well who treat us well, but if we are kind to someone who would qualify as an enemy, it is then that we are really showing love (see Luke 6:32–35).

People are always going to be part of our lives, and not all of them are pleasant. Will you act on the Word of God and love them for His sake? If you do, you'll be amazed at how much it will help them...and how much it will help you.

Today's Thought

In your quiet time with God, take time to pray for those in your life who may be hard to get along with. Turn those people over to God and trust Him to do a healing work in their hearts.

Dig Deeper into God's Word: Study Matthew 5:44; Romans 12:14

Go to God First

So we take comfort and are encouraged and confidently say, "The Lord is my Helper [in time of need], I will not be afraid." (Hebrews 13:6)

The fact that God is a help to us should fill us with great calm and confidence. Anytime there is a decision to be made, we can go to God and ask for His guidance and direction. After all, the Word promises that He will help us.

So many people wait and go to God as a last resort. After they have tried everything they can think of, or after they have made a decision that didn't work out, then they go to God in a panic and beg for help. But that is a backward process. That's like going out and buying a coat on the last day of winter.

No matter how big or small the decision you are facing, ask God for His wisdom. Ask Him to show you what to do and when to do it...and then believe He is leading you as you go forward.

Today's Thought

Rather than going to God as a last resort, make it a practice to seek Him first thing each day and in each situation.

Dig Deeper into God's Word: Study 2 Corinthians 8:5;
     1 Peter 3:18

The Battle Is the Lord's

With us is the Lord our God to help us and to fight our battles. (2 Chronicles 32:8)

I wish more people understood the power of godly determination. I hear from individuals all the time who have given up. The battle got too intense, and somewhere along the way, they just stopped fighting. Like Peter, who put his focus on the wind and the waves instead of Jesus, they've put their focus on the turmoil in their lives instead of Jesus, and it has caused them to be afraid.

If you've ever felt that way—overwhelmed and tempted to give up—let me remind you that God has promised to fight your battles for you. The key to determination is to realize you are not alone. You are not called to win in your own strength; God wins in *His* strength. Bring any and every problem to God and lay them at His feet. God goes before you, and the battle belongs to Him.

Today's Thought

Perseverance is never about confidence and determination that you have the strength to win; it is always about confidence and determination that God has the strength to win.

Dig Deeper into God's Word: Study 1 Samuel 17:47; Proverbs 21:31

The Goodness and Loving-Kindness of God

The goodness and kindness of God our Savior and His love for mankind appeared [in human form as the Man, Jesus Christ]. (Titus 3:4)

God is good—all the time. His goodness radiates from Him because that is who He is. If you were hurt or neglected in your childhood, or wounded deeply by someone in your life, you might be wondering why, if God is good, He didn't deliver you from those circumstances. I understand that question, because I've asked it many times myself.

I don't always get all the answers I would like to have, but I have learned to trust God even when I feel like I am in the dark. I've learned that even if we can't see it at the time, God is still good, and He can restore any situation.

God's entire motive and purpose is to do good to you if you will only receive it from Him. Don't let a past pain take your eyes off of the Lord. In your quiet time with Him, ask God for His help and wait expectantly for His goodness to bring joy and peace to your life.

Today's Thought

Perhaps not everything that has happened in your life is good, but God is for you, and He can work it out for good if you trust Him.

Dig Deeper into God's Word: Study Psalm 145:9; Jeremiah 33:11

Waiting on the Lord

But those who wait for the Lord [who expect, look for, and hope in Him] will gain new strength and renew their power. (Isaiah 40:31)

What does it really mean to wait for the Lord? It simply means spending time with Him, being in His presence, meditating on His Word, worshipping Him, and keeping Him at the center of our lives. One meaning of the word *wait* (translated from *qavah* in Hebrew) is "to bind together by twisting; to become braided together."

Think about it: A braid is woven together so that you cannot tell where one strand ends and another begins. That is the way God wants us to be in our union with Him.

An intimate relationship with God will strengthen you in the innermost part of your being. When you wait on the Lord, you draw everything you need from Him. He is your refuge, your enabler, your joy, your peace, your righteousness, and your hope. He gives you everything you need to live in victory over any circumstance.

Today's Thought

As we wait on the Lord, we become more and more like Him—so tightly woven together with Him that we are one with Him, that we are direct representatives of His character.

Dig Deeper into God's Word: Study Psalm 62:1;
    Psalm 25:5

Be the Blessing Someone Needs

*Do not merely look out for your own personal interests, but
also for the interests of others. (Philippians 2:4)*

Every person needs help. We all need to be encouraged, edified,
and appreciated. And you can be that blessing someone else needs.
God not only wants to bless your life, but He wants you to be a
blessing to those around you. Everyone grows weary at times and
needs other people to say to them, "I just wanted to let you know
that I appreciate you and all you do."

I believe God blesses us so we can be a blessing—not only in a
few places, but everywhere we go. Look for people who are in need
and bless them. Share what you have with those who are less fortunate than you are, give an encouraging word, and be kind. When
you live to meet needs and encourage those around you, you will
find "joy unspeakable" in the process (see 1 Peter 1:8 KJV).

Today's Thought

*You are God's representative to the world around you. Just
like Jesus, go through your day looking to do good. When
you do, you'll make the world a better place, one kind act
at a time.*

Dig Deeper into God's Word: Study Hebrews 13:16;
    Galatians 6:2

Growing in Spiritual Maturity

But grow [spiritually mature] in the grace and knowledge of our Lord and Savior Jesus Christ. To Him be glory (honor, majesty, splendor), both now and to the day of eternity. Amen. (2 Peter 3:18)

Spiritual maturity isn't developed by merely going to church and hearing great sermons—it is the result of learning and applying the Word of God in your everyday life.

The Word of God, when it is received and becomes rooted in our hearts, has the power to change us from the inside out. When we study God's Word, meditate on His promises, and then do what it teaches us, we mature spiritually.

Doing the right thing when it hurts or is hard to do brings about spiritual growth. The more we grow, the more we are able to do challenging things with ease.

Today's Thought

Study the Word of God and put what you learn into practice in your life.

Dig Deeper into God's Word: Study 1 Peter 2:2; Ephesians 4:15–16

Your Body, God's Temple

Do you not know that your body is a temple of the Holy Spirit who is within you, whom you have [received as a gift] from God, and that you are not your own [property]? (1 Corinthians 6:19)

God created us as tripart beings (spirit, soul, and body). We have many facets to our nature, and each needs proper care. If we don't take good care of our bodies, our spirit and soul will be less effective. If we rarely exercise, rest, or eat properly, it will cause our health to suffer.

I have discovered that when I feel tired and worn-out, it becomes difficult for me to maintain the spiritual disciplines that I need to do in order to stay strong in spirit and soul. Good health and energy help us in every way, even spiritually.

Your body is the residence of your spirit and soul; it is the house they dwell in while on this earth. Not only that, God's Word says that your body is the very temple of God. I encourage you to take care of it each and every day.

Today's Thought

Take care of your body, because it is the only one you will ever have.

Dig Deeper into God's Word: Study Romans 12:1; 1 Corinthians 3:16–17

Healed and Whole

Beloved, I pray that in every way you may succeed and prosper and be in good health [physically], just as [I know] your soul prospers [spiritually]. (3 John 1:2)

Pain from our past has a way of hanging around. Childhood traumas and other emotional wounds often linger in our minds. For many people, these memories hold them back in life.

But that doesn't have to be you. The good news is that, in Christ, you are not broken or fractured—you are healed and whole. You can move past the effects of previous wounds and go on to do great things.

Anytime you are reminded of how you were wounded, think about how much God loves you. You're not damaged or inferior because someone or something hurt you. You are a loved, redeemed, restored child of God.

Knowing how valuable you are to God and that He has an amazing plan for your life will enable you to overcome painful memories and embrace the love and joy of God that are yours today.

Today's Thought

Jesus died to bring you complete healing—in your spirit, soul, and body. Receive His healing touch in every area of your life.

Dig Deeper into God's Word: Study Psalm 147:3;
    Isaiah 53:5

Moving Past "Can't"

What then shall we say to all these things? If God is for us, who can be [successful] against us? (Romans 8:31)

I can't is one of the most harmful phrases you can ever mutter. And I believe God wants to help you break free from the cage of *can't*. You *can* receive hope today, maybe for the first time. Whatever challenge or opportunity lies before you, you *can* succeed—because God is with you, and He will give you all the strength you need.

Negative words from others are no match for the promises of God and His presence in your life. When God is for you, it doesn't matter who or what is against you.

Let God build your confidence moving forward. You may have failed in the past, but you *can* overcome today. You may have made mistakes in the past, but you *can* make wise decisions today. You may have given up in the past, but you *can* persevere today. With God's help, you *can* do it!

Today's Thought

If you think you can't, then you won't, but if you think you can, then you will.

Dig Deeper into God's Word: Study Philippians 4:13; 2 Corinthians 4:16–17

There Is Always Hope

And now, Lord, for what do I expectantly wait? My hope [my confident expectation] is in You. (Psalm 39:7)

It's easy to look at your struggles in life and get discouraged. If you look only at your obstacles, it's easy to lose hope. Maybe you've been diagnosed with a serious illness and feel you won't recover. You might look at your bank account and feel hopeless. You may drive to work and think, *There's no hope for a promotion.* And that is exactly what the devil wants you to do. He knows that if he can keep you hopeless, you cannot move on with bold faith, and you'll miss God's great plan for your life.

Resist the temptation to look at what you have lost or don't have—choose to look at all that God has done, is doing, and will do. When you do, hope will come alive, joy will increase, and your faith will grow. When you live in the garden of hope, something is always blooming. Instead of believing the lie that things are hopeless, choose to declare, "With God, there is always hope!"

Today's Thought

The more you focus on what God has already done in your life, the more you will have hope for what He will do in your future.

Dig Deeper into God's Word: Study Romans 15:13; 1 Timothy 4:10

Speaking God's Promises over Your Life

Fight the good fight of the faith; lay hold of the eternal life to which you were summoned and [for which] you confessed the good confession [of faith] before many witnesses.
(1 Timothy 6:12 AMPC)

One of the most important things you can do in your quiet time with God is to stand in agreement with Him and His Word. For example, no matter how you feel, agree with God that He loves you. You are wonderfully made and have many gifts and talents. You are valuable, and as a believer in Jesus, you are the righteousness of God in Him.

Speak out against feelings of doubt and insecurity by saying, "I am God's workmanship!" Come into agreement with God about you and your future, and say what He says in His Word.

1 Timothy 6:12 tells us to fight the good fight, and one way to do that is to speak God's truth over your life. So fight the good fight of faith and refuse to live below the level where Jesus wants you to live. Use your words to get in agreement with God about who you are and about the promises that are yours as a child of Almighty God.

Today's Thought

There is tremendous power in the words you speak. Refuse to speak words of self-pity or insecurity.

Dig Deeper into God's Word: Study Ephesians 2:10;
   Romans 10:9

Tests and Trials

Beloved, do not be surprised at the fiery ordeal which is taking place to test you [that is, to test the quality of your faith], as though something strange or unusual were happening to you. (1 Peter 4:12)

No one who does anything worthwhile for God has traveled an easy road. Doing great things for God requires character, and character is developed by passing life's tests and staying faithful to Him through trials.

One reason God allows us to go through tests and trials is to show us weak areas in our lives. Until they are exposed, we cannot do anything about them. But once we see them, we can begin to face them and ask God to help us. God allows us to walk through difficult times so we will recognize our need for Him. Never be afraid of the truth, because it is the truth that makes us free (see John 8:32).

The next time you encounter some sort of test or trial, determine to believe it will work out for your good. Say to God, "I believe this is going to work out well for me. I don't understand it all right now, but I believe You will use it for my ultimate good."

Today's Thought

God cares about everything that concerns you, and He is always working for your good.

Dig Deeper into God's Word: Study 1 Corinthians 10:13; 1 Peter 5:8–9

Putting on the Armor of God

*Put on the full armor of God [for His precepts are like the
splendid armor of a heavily-armed soldier], so that you may
be able to [successfully] stand up against all the schemes and
the strategies and the deceits of the devil. (Ephesians 6:11)*

You have been equipped and empowered to overcome any attack
of the enemy. You have been given the armor of God! But the Bible
says that you must *put on* that armor—this is a conscious decision
on your part.

I suggest you take a few minutes in your quiet time with God
each morning and pray, *Lord, today I put on the armor You have provided for me through Jesus. I thank You that I am righteous today in
Christ. I choose to wear the breastplate of righteousness. And I thank
You that I have the shield of faith. Today I will choose to live by faith,
not by sight, trusting the promises in Your Word. Also, I thank You that
You have armed me with the sword of the Spirit.*

Then go through the list of armor found in Ephesians 6:13–17,
piece by piece. Declaring these promises out loud helps renew your
mind, helps release the blessings of God that are yours, and helps
you stand against any attack of the enemy.

Today's Thought

*You are not helpless, you are not weak, and you are not a
victim. You are a warrior in the army of God!*

Dig Deeper into God's Word: Study Isaiah 59:17; 1
    Peter 3:15

Change the Conversation

Death and life are in the power of the tongue, and those who love it and indulge it will eat its fruit and bear the consequences of their words. (Proverbs 18:21)

Rather than rehearse your problems, you can use today's quiet time with God to start reciting His goodness.

Talking excessively about our cares or concerns does nothing to make them go away. All talking about our problems does is maximize stress. The more we talk about everything that could go wrong, the more we are turning up the volume on stress and turning down the volume on faith.

But something amazing happens when we change the conversation. When we begin talking about the power, goodness, and faithfulness of God in spite of our problems, our stress levels decrease.

It's not that our words instantly change the circumstances we're facing, but they have the power to change our attitude about those circumstances until the circumstances do change.

Today's Thought

If your conversations are positive, hope-filled, and full of encouragement, you will face the day with joy and optimism.

Dig Deeper into God's Word: Study Proverbs 10:11; Ephesians 4:29

In the World but Not of the World

They are not of the world and do not belong to the world, just as I am not of the world and do not belong to it. (John 17:14)

It often seems like we are surrounded by problems in this life, but the good news is that as Christians, though we may be *in* the world, according to John 17:14–16, we are not *of* the world. We don't have to operate by the world's system, reacting like the world. Our attitude and approach can be totally different.

The world responds to difficulties by being frustrated and upset, but Jesus said in John 14:27, "Peace I leave with you; My [perfect] peace I give to you; not as the world gives do I give to you."

This verse indicates we can have a change of perspective. The right mindset and the right attitude can completely turn a situation around. If we approach something with dread, we're setting ourselves up for misery. But if we refuse to dread or have a negative outlook, we open the door for God to work supernaturally and help us. We can choose our own perspective.

Today's Thought

Because Jesus has deprived the world of its power to harm us, we can approach the challenges we face in life with a new perspective—in a calm and confident manner.

Dig Deeper into God's Word: Study John 15:19; 1 John 2:16

Joy in the Midst of Sorrow

*You have turned my mourning into dancing for me; You have
taken off my sackcloth and clothed me with joy. (Psalm 30:11)*

If you are experiencing emotional or physical pain—no matter how
big or how small—it can seem overwhelming. But here is something to hold on to: a struggle or personal loss doesn't have to over-
shadow every part of your life. You can still have joy even in the
midst of sorrow.

Joy isn't always extreme hilarity; sometimes joy is simply a calm
delight. And you can delight yourself in God and in His promise to
always be with you (see Deuteronomy 31:6) even when times are
difficult—*especially* when times are difficult.

The key is to trust God. He knows what you're going through,
and if you trust Him, He will restore your joy. You may not see how
it's going to work out or how you're going to get over it, but know
that God is in control, and He can do the impossible.

Today's Thought

God is with you at all times, and He is working in your life.

Dig Deeper into God's Word: Study Psalm 31:7;
    John 16:22

Resurrection Power

Jesus said to her, "Did I not say to you that if you believe [in Me], you will see the glory of God [the expression of His excellence]?" (John 11:40)

When Lazarus died, his sister Martha was in a state of despair. Jesus told her, "Your brother will rise [from the dead]," but Martha replied, "I know that he will rise [from the dead] in the resurrection on the last day" (John 11:23–24). She didn't really understand what Jesus was saying. She was looking for something in the future; she didn't expect things to change in the present.

A lot of times, we are like Martha in this way. We think we are stuck in our problems, not realizing that God can turn things around. Jesus raised Lazarus from the dead, and He can raise the "Lazaruses" in your life, too. Whether you need Him to restore a relationship, give you a breakthrough in your health, or remove an obstacle that is in the way of His plan for your life—He can do it all! Don't get stuck in despair; stand in faith and have an expectant heart for God's power to be revealed today.

Today's Thought

Expect God to do something amazing in your life.

Dig Deeper into God's Word: Study John 6:40; 1 Corinthians 6:14

Defeating the Enemy

*But thanks be to God, who always leads us in triumph
in Christ, and through us spreads and makes evident
everywhere the sweet fragrance of the knowledge of Him.
(2 Corinthians 2:14)*

The enemy cannot hold you back if you are determined. You will
have to be more determined than he is, but you can do it, because
God is on your side. The enemy may oppose you fiercely, but you
can defeat him and achieve your goals in life if you simply refuse to
give up.

Some people become afraid at the thought that the enemy is
against them, but there is no need to fear. God is on your side, and
He always leads you in triumph.

To defeat the devil, take time regularly to seek God, study His
Word, worship Him, and pray. Let your requests be made known to
God, but don't worry about the problem. Trust God to do battle on
your behalf. The Word of God tells us that the battle is the Lord's
(see 2 Chronicles 20:15). If you refuse to give up, there is no way
you can lose, because God is undefeated!

Today's Thought

*Pray at all times, not just when you face a crisis. We need
God not just in the midst of disasters; we need Him all the
time.*

Dig Deeper into God's Word: Study Romans 8:37; 1
    Chronicles 29:11

Be Steadfast and Diligent

*"In the world you have tribulation and distress and suf-
fering, but be courageous [be confident, be undaunted, be
filled with joy]; I have overcome the world." [My conquest
is accomplished, My victory abiding.] (John 16:33)*

Many people live lives far short of God's best because they expect
things to always be convenient or easy. But this false expectation will always cheat us out of the rewards God has for us simply
because we want to avoid difficulty.

Jesus never promised things would be easy, but He did promise us victory, because He has overcome the world. If we don't get
weary of doing what is right, we will reap great benefits.

God is a loving Father, and He wants to bless you in so many
ways. Sometimes you may go through difficulties first, but there
are always blessings on the other side. Remember, you can always
rely on His strength to see you through, because He has overcome
the world.

Today's Thought

*If you refuse to give up, with God's help, you'll overcome
every challenge and receive God's best for your life.*

Dig Deeper into God's Word: Study Proverbs 8:17;
    Proverbs 4:23

You Have a Guide

But when He, the Spirit of Truth, comes, He will guide you into all the truth [full and complete truth]. For He will not speak on His own initiative, but He will speak whatever He hears [from the Father—the message regarding the Son], and He will disclose to you what is to come [in the future]. (John 16:13)

Making decisions can be a very stressful thing if you are expected to make them on your own, but thankfully, you're not. It is so comforting to know that God has given us His Holy Spirit to guide us through life.

You can be at peace about making decisions, knowing that you are not expected to make them on your own. Not only is God with you, but He is also going to give you the guidance you need to make a wise choice.

John 16:13 says that the Holy Spirit "will guide you into all the truth." The fact that the Holy Spirit is your guide makes all the difference. Don't be stressed out by the choices you face today. Stay in peace, and expect to hear clearly from God.

Today's Thought

You are not traveling through life alone. The Holy Spirit is your guide, and He promises to give you wisdom and lead you into all truth.

Dig Deeper into God's Word: Study Psalm 5:8;
    Romans 8:14

Praying a Difficult Prayer

Bless and show kindness to those who curse you, pray for
those who mistreat you. (Luke 6:28)

When someone hurts our feelings, the last thing we want to do
is actually pray for them. But this is what God instructs us to do.
God's Word says that when people mistreat us, we must pray for
them and bless them (see Luke 6:28).

It's not a natural response to pray for someone who has hurt us,
but God's wisdom is higher than ours, so even though it doesn't
feel right, it is the right thing to do. Be willing to pray in obedience:
Lord, I don't really feel like praying for that person who hurt me, but
in obedience to Your Word, I'm doing it anyway. I pray Your best for
their life.

God instructs us to practice forgiveness. And when we choose to
follow the path of forgiveness, we will experience the peace and joy
that come through obeying God's Word.

Today's Thought

When you obey God, regardless of whether you feel like it
or not, He can help you overcome the pain of offense and
enjoy life more.

Dig Deeper into God's Word: Study 1 Peter 3:9;
      Mark 11:25

God Promises to Forgive

To the Lord our God belong mercy and lovingkindness and forgiveness. (Daniel 9:9)

In the Old Testament, we see many instances where the Israelites would complain, disobey, or worship idols and false gods. But I am always amazed at how quickly God completely forgave them. When they repented, He restored all of His benefits to them as soon as they turned back to Him.

Many people feel that God is angry with them—He is not! God is ready and willing to completely forgive our sins. He understands we have weaknesses, and He knows we are going to miss the mark from time to time. But God is a compassionate, loving Father who has provided for our forgiveness in Christ. All we need to do is ask for that forgiveness and then receive it.

The very fact that we are imperfect and prone to sin is why God sent Jesus to pay the price for our redemption. God is not angry with you. Choose to accept and walk in His forgiveness today.

Today's Thought

Don't allow your faults or your sins to drive you away from God. Choose to receive His forgiveness and know that He removes your sin as far as the east is from the west.

Dig Deeper into God's Word: Study 1 John 1:9; Matthew 6:14

Praying at All Times

*With all prayer and petition pray [with specific requests]
at all times [on every occasion and in every season] in the
Spirit, and with this in view, stay alert with all perseverance and petition [interceding in prayer] for all God's people. (Ephesians 6:18)*

When we read this scripture that tells us to pray "at all times," we
often wonder, *Lord, how can I ever get to the place that I am able to
pray without ceasing?* (See 1 Thessalonians 5:17.) We may think the
phrase *without ceasing* means nonstop, without ever quitting. How
is that possible?

But what Paul is saying is that prayer should be like breathing,
something we do all the time to sustain ourselves. Our physical
bodies require breathing, and our spiritual lives are fed and nur-
tured by consistent communication with God.

Prayer can be as simple as lifting up your heart to God and whis-
pering, "Thank You." You can pray anywhere, at any time. It does
not require that we be in a special posture or talk to God at a special time, and it doesn't even need to be long; it just needs to be
sincere. Realizing this will help you pray more often.

Today's Thought

*God is always listening, and He wants to be part of every-
thing that you do.*

Dig Deeper into God's Word: Study 1 Thessalonians
    5:17; Luke 11:1–4

Believe the Best in Every Situation

If there is any excellence, if there is anything worthy of praise, think continually on these things [center your mind on them, and implant them in your heart]. (Philippians 4:8)

One of the best things you can do is think good and excellent thoughts, especially about other people.

That's not always easy to do. It's natural to find fault and assign blame—our flesh (human nature without God) does that automatically. But seeing and believing the best is a choice. It's a decision you make to change the default setting in your life from negative to positive.

Instead of assuming the worst, believe the best. Believe the best about your co-worker. Believe the best about your church. Believe the best about your spouse and children. Believe the best about your health. Believe the best about your future. You'd be amazed at how your entire outlook will change by simply believing the best about the people and situations in your life.

Today's Thought

What you believe and think about is your choice, so why not make it something that is good?

Dig Deeper into God's Word: Study Ephesians 4:31–32; Joshua 1:9

Hope or Cynicism

Constantly rejoicing in hope [because of our confidence in Christ], steadfast and patient in distress, devoted to prayer [continually seeking wisdom, guidance, and strength].
(Romans 12:12)

Hope and cynicism can't coexist. This is why it is so important to have a good attitude about the people in your life and the tasks you face from day to day. When you do, hope thrives and cynicism dies.

If you say goodbye to a critical spirit and a complaining attitude, you'll discover an exciting new level of joy. You'll begin to appreciate the people you once took for granted, and you'll begin to see daily tasks as opportunities rather than obligations.

Most people who are unhappy in life are focusing on unhappy things. They talk about everything that is wrong, and they generally have a negative disposition. Hope does the opposite. That is why hope brings happiness. When you are expecting God to do something good, you can't help but be happy.

Today's Thought

Think happy! Be happy!

Dig Deeper into God's Word: Study Lamentations 3:24; Ephesians 1:18

Intimacy with God

Come close to God [with a contrite heart] and He will come close to you. (James 4:8)

Jesus did not die for us to give us a religion, but to open the way for each of us to have and enjoy an intimate relationship with God through Him. Religious people tend to focus on following rules and laws, but those seeking a relationship with God focus on Him.

Each of us can be as close to God as we want to be; it all depends on how much time we are willing to put into developing our relationship with Him.

Form a habit of spending regular quiet time with God, studying His Word, and talking with Him. If you put Him first, He will help you be obedient to His will. Don't make the mistake of thinking that you don't have time to spend with God, because it is the single most important thing that you can do.

Today's Thought

If you are too busy to spend time with God, then you are definitely too busy!

Dig Deeper into God's Word: Study John 3:16–17; Jeremiah 33:3

There Is So Much to Be Grateful For

Be thankful and say so to Him, bless and affectionately praise His name! (Psalm 100:4 AMPC)

Gratitude is a powerful thing. Not only does it help set us free, but as we pause to give thanks to God for the blessings we enjoy in our lives, we actually begin to find more blessings—even *more* to be thankful for!

David said, "I will bless the Lord at all times; His praise shall continually be in my mouth...Many hardships and perplexing circumstances confront the righteous, but the Lord rescues him from them all" (Psalm 34:1, 19). What a great example of praise and thankfulness!

In your quiet time with God and all throughout each day, I encourage you to take moments to practice being thankful. There is so much for us to be grateful for, and we need to focus on those things every single day.

Today's Thought

Praising God is simply recognizing His awesome power and thanking Him for His amazing goodness in your life.

Dig Deeper into God's Word: Study Hebrews 12:28; Colossians 3:17

The Battle Within

For the sinful nature has its desire which is opposed to the Spirit, and the [desire of the] Spirit opposes the sinful nature; for these [two, the sinful nature and the Spirit] are in direct opposition to each other [continually in conflict]. (Galatians 5:17)

The flesh and the spirit are at battle with each other. We may have an impulse or a sense about something, and we know in our hearts it is right, but our minds will try to talk us out of it. This happens in all of us.

Let's say you sense you should give money to a family in need. Your heart believes it is the right thing to do, and you believe it will please God because this desire is inspired by the Holy Spirit. But your flesh might say, *Don't give anything to those people; they have never done anything for you.* The flesh fights against the spirit, and you struggle to decide which one to listen to.

I am convinced we miss many blessings in our lives because we try to mentally understand too much instead of simply allowing the Holy Spirit to lead us. Do what is in your heart, not your head. Do what you have peace about doing, not just what you want to do.

Today's Thought

As you follow the Holy Spirit and His leading in your heart (your spirit), you will invest in tomorrow by making the right choices today.

Dig Deeper into God's Word: Study Romans 8:13; 1 Peter 2:11

God Is Your Vindicator

For we know Him who said, "Vengeance is Mine [retribution and the deliverance of justice rest with Me], I will repay [the wrongdoer]." (Hebrews 10:30)

Wow! This is a wonderful and comforting scripture, and if you are suffering due to unjust treatment from someone else, you should hide this scripture in your heart and trust God to be your vindicator.

To be compensated for an injustice means you are paid back for what happened to you. There is nothing sweeter than watching God honor and bless you because someone has treated you unfairly. But we have to give up trying to make others pay us back for the injustices we've endured if we want to see God vindicate us.

God requires us to let go of the past and forgive our enemies completely, to pray for them and even bless them as He leads us in how to do that. If you forgive those who hurt you, God will protect you and bring about justice in your life.

Today's Thought

No matter how deep or intense a problem may be, God is always bigger, and He can heal it, work good out of it, and recompense you for past pain.

Dig Deeper into God's Word: Study Romans 12:19; 1 Samuel 24:12

Being Obedient While You Wait on God

Wait for and expect the Lord and keep His way, and He will exalt you to inherit the land; [in the end] when the wicked are cut off, you will see it. (Psalm 37:34)

Obedience to God isn't always easy, especially when we find ourselves in God's waiting room, enduring difficult circumstances. Displaying the fruit of the Spirit is much more challenging when we have stress and pressure in our lives. It can even be difficult to pray or study God's Word; however, these are the times when it is the most important to do so.

Doing the right thing while the right thing is not happening to us is possibly one of the most powerful things that we can do. Paul tells us not to be weary in doing what is right, for in due time we shall reap if we don't faint (see Galatians 6:9).

Keep doing what is right while you are in God's waiting room. Do it because you love Him and because you appreciate all that He has done and is doing for you even right now.

Today's Thought

God always sees faithfulness even if no one else does. And those who remain steadfast during trials will receive the victor's crown of life (see James 1:12).

Dig Deeper into God's Word: Study James 5:7–8; Psalm 37:7

Step Out and Try

*A man's mind plans his way [as he journeys through life],
but the Lord directs his steps and establishes them. (Proverbs 16:9)*

People often ask me how they can determine God's will for their
lives. Many people spend years waiting to hear a voice or to receive
a supernatural sign giving them direction. But receiving direction
from God is usually more practical than that. So my advice is: *Step
out and find out.*

Early in my Christian life, I wanted to serve God but didn't
know exactly what to do. When different opportunities would
arise, I would try those things that were available. A lot of them
didn't work out for me, but I kept trying until I found an area that
fit me. I came alive inside when I had an opportunity to teach the
Word of God, and I knew that was what I was supposed to do.

Sometimes the only way to discover the will of God is to practice
"stepping out and finding out." If you have prayed about a situation
and don't seem to know what you should do, take a step of faith.
Even if that is not God's ultimate destination, it will be another step
toward the fulfillment of His will for your life.

Today's Thought

*Don't be afraid of making a mistake. God sees your heart
and knows that you have pure motives. Step out in faith, and
God will guide you.*

Dig Deeper into God's Word: Study 2 Corinthians 5:7;
    Ecclesiastes 11:6

The Choice to Live Amazed

And they were surprised [almost overwhelmed] at His teaching, because His message was [given] with authority and power and great ability. (Luke 4:32)

There are many days in life when we let what should be extremely special to us become too average or ordinary.

I remember a time years ago when I was praying and said, "Lord, why don't I have those exciting, special things happening in my life like I used to when I first started to know You?"

I'll never forget what the Lord spoke to my heart so clearly. He said, "Joyce, I still do the same things all the time; it's just that you've gotten used to them." *Wow!*

If we will determine to stay amazed at the things God is doing in our lives—even the little things—we'll be much more encouraged and refreshed in our walk with God. In your quiet times, take the opportunity to realize what you have, be thankful, and decide to live amazed at His faithfulness and goodness.

Today's Thought

God's blessings are all around you. All you have to do is look for them and you will be amazed at all He has done for you.

Dig Deeper into God's Word: Study Psalm 33:8; Psalm 19:1

Refreshed and Renewed

Even youths grow weary and tired, and vigorous young men stumble badly, but those who wait for the Lord [who expect, look for, and hope in Him] will gain new strength and renew their power. (Isaiah 40:30–31)

No one is exempt from the need for renewal; everyone needs times of rest, refreshment, and restoration.

When you feel extremely weary, it is important to be careful. Weary people often make emotional decisions, say things without thinking, take shortcuts they later regret, and settle for less than the best because they are tired and worn-out.

I'm convinced that we will make much better choices in life if we will simply spend time with God on a regular basis. If we will seek God, we will hear from Him.

Begin to take time to wait on God and allow Him to renew your strength. Take breaks as soon as you feel weary and say, "I love You, Lord. I need You. I feel a little weary today. Please strengthen me."

Today's Thought

Honoring God by giving Him special, set-apart time will produce great results in our lives and bring restoration and refreshment to our souls.

Dig Deeper into God's Word: Study Psalm 51:10;
  Matthew 11:28–29

The Right to Feel Good

*He made Christ who knew no sin to [judicially] be sin on
our behalf, so that in Him we would become the righteousness of God [that is, we would be made acceptable to Him
and placed in a right relationship with Him by His gracious lovingkindness]. (2 Corinthians 5:21)*

Jesus paid for your freedom with His own blood. He purchased you,
made you right and acceptable to Him, and set you free from bondage to sin and guilt. You don't have to live with a guilty conscience
and bad feelings about yourself because you make mistakes. You
can appreciate who God has made you to be and learn how to love
yourself—not in a selfish, self-centered way, but in a godly way,
because He loves you.

Self-rejection leads to all kinds of other problems. God loves us, so
we can love ourselves, not in a haughty way, but in a healthy, balanced,
biblical way, because we believe Christ, who knew no sin, became sin
for us so we might be made the righteousness of God in Him.

We have no right to reject what God purchased with the blood
of His Son, our Lord and Savior, Jesus Christ. God loves us, and we
need to agree with Him, not with the devil, who tries to make us
feel worthless. Start today loving the person God created you to be!

Today's Thought

*You are valuable, you are talented and gifted, and God has
a special purpose for you.*

Dig Deeper into God's Word: Study Romans 8:1–2;
    Hebrews 10:22

Making You Stronger

Do not fear [anything], for I am with you; do not be afraid, for I am your God. I will strengthen you, be assured I will help you; I will certainly take hold of you with My righteous right hand [a hand of justice, of power, of victory, of salvation]. (Isaiah 41:10)

In the book of Isaiah, we see God speaking through the prophet to the people and encouraging them not to fear what they were going through because He was going to use it to make them stronger.

This is another example of God's promise to use what we go through to make us more mature and better than we were before. But this all hinges on whether or not we are willing to put our total trust in God concerning painful things we encounter in life.

Whatever you might be going through right now, this promise is for you. Your enemies may mean harm, but God will work it out for good, and in the process, He will make you a better person.

Today's Thought

When life is painful and hard, remember that God loves you, and because of that you don't have to be afraid.

Dig Deeper into God's Word: Study 2 Corinthians
    12:10; Isaiah 40:31

Never Give Up on Your Future

"For I know the plans and thoughts that I have for you,"
says the Lord, "plans for peace and well-being and not for
disaster, to give you a future and a hope." (Jeremiah 29:11)

Never giving up means marching into your future with boldness
and confidence, seeing each new day as an opportunity to move
forward in the best God has for you and taking each new challenge as a mountain to be climbed instead of a boulder that will
crush you.

You have a great future ahead of you, but you will not be able to
fully enter into it and enjoy it if your past still holds you captive.
The past has the potential to keep you from experiencing the joy,
freedom, and blessings of the present and the future—*but only if
you let it.*

God wants you to set your face toward your future with hope,
courage, and expectation. And the best way I know to never give up
on your future is to refuse to be trapped in your past.

Today's Thought

Don't let the past steal the life you have today and the
future you have tomorrow. You have to let go in order to
go on.

Dig Deeper into God's Word: Study Romans 8:28;
Isaiah 43:18–19

Keep Smiling

Consider it nothing but joy, my brothers and sisters, whenever you fall into various trials. Be assured that the testing of your faith [through experience] produces endurance [leading to spiritual maturity, and inner peace]. (James 1:2–3)

Whatever unexpected challenge or frustration you may face, decide in advance that you're not going to let it steal your joy in your quiet time with God. Being unhappy does nothing except make you miserable, so don't waste your time with it.

- If your child wakes up with a cold and can't go to school, choose to have a positive outlook. Thank God it's just a cold and nothing worse.
- If the dry cleaner ruins one of your outfits, choose to have a positive outlook. Now you have an excuse to go shopping.
- If you lose your job, choose to be positive. Now you have the opportunity to get a better job.

Don't let the daily events of life determine your mindset, attitudes, and behavior. Instead, let the goodness of God and the promises in His Word set the direction for your life.

Today's Thought

You can't change a negative circumstance by being negative, so stay positive and expect God to do something amazing.

Dig Deeper into God's Word: Study Romans 5:3; 2
   Corinthians 4:17

What Are You Saying?

*A man has joy in giving an appropriate answer, and how
good and delightful is a word spoken at the right moment—
how good it is! (Proverbs 15:23)*

You've probably heard someone say, "You might end up eating those
words." It may sound like a simple expression to us, but in reality
we do eat our words. What we say not only affects our friends and
the people around us, but it also profoundly affects us. The question
is, how will your words impact your life: positively or negatively?

Words are wonderful when used in a proper way. They can
encourage, edify, and give confidence to the hearer. A right word
spoken at the right time can be used to change a life.

You can increase your own joy and greatly reduce stress by
speaking the right words. You can also upset yourself by talking
unnecessarily about your problems or about things that have hurt
you. The choice is yours to make today and every day.

Today's Thought

*Talk more about what God is doing in your life than you do
about your problems.*

Dig Deeper into God's Word: Study Psalm 141:3;
    Isaiah 50:4

Heartfelt and Persistent Prayer

The heartfelt and persistent prayer of a righteous man (believer) can accomplish much [when put into action and made effective by God—it is dynamic and can have tremendous power]. (James 5:16)

Prayer is passionate. It's about sincerity of heart and putting your whole heart into it. Prayer doesn't have to be eloquent or long. And prayer isn't better if it's loud or if you're folding your hands or bowing your head. It's good to humble yourself, but it's not your posture or how long you pray that makes it effective.

I remember a time when God challenged me to ask for what I wanted and needed in the fewest number of words possible. This was hard at first. But He began to show me that it's not about how many words we say; it's about the heart behind those words.

The Bible says that faith pleases God (Hebrews 11:6), and if we believe He exists and seek Him, He will reward us. We don't have to beg and plead with Him to help us. God is a good God! He loves you and wants what is best for you.

Today's Thought

Prayer is a powerful privilege, so pray often.

Dig Deeper into God's Word: Study 1 John 5:14;
    Luke 11:9–10

Right Choices

I have set before you life and death, the blessing and the curse; therefore, you shall choose life in order that you may live, you and your descendants. (Deuteronomy 30:19)

Allowing our emotions to lead our decisions will definitely prevent us from having a life filled with peace and joy. Emotional decisions almost always cause turmoil.

The law of God's kingdom is that we reap what we sow (see Galatians 6:7). If we choose to sow discipline and right choices, we will reap a life of joy and contentment. However, if we sow choices based solely on how we feel, we will reap a life of frustration, regret, and sadness.

God sets before every person life and death, and He instructs us to choose life. Since we all have the privilege of free will, we must take responsibility for our lives and no longer blame circumstances and other people for the choices we make. Instead, we can ask God to give us the discipline and wisdom to make right choices each day.

Today's Thought

We can't be led by our emotions and be led by the Holy Spirit. We have to make a choice which one to follow.

Dig Deeper into God's Word: Study Galatians 5:13; Joshua 24:15

God Isn't in a Rush

My times are in Your hands. (Psalm 31:15)

We have instant credit approval, instant oatmeal, instant coffee, and drive-through everything. We like to think God's ways are the same, but they are not. God is not in a rush, and there's no such thing as a "drive-through breakthrough."

The psalmist said it this way: "My times are in Your hands." This was the prayer of a man in a desperate situation. His enemies were out to kill him. Still, he didn't panic; he trusted God's timing.

Your life and your times are also in God's hands. If you're facing delays and have to wait, God knows. He's the One who controls the clock of your life. Don't focus only on reaching your desired destination. Focus on the journey, and be determined to enjoy each phase of it.

Today's Thought

God will not be rushed, but what He does will be perfect!

Dig Deeper into God's Word: Study Ecclesiastes 3:1; Acts 1:7

Working All Things for Your Good

To grant to those who mourn in Zion... the oil of joy instead of mourning, the garment [expressive] of praise instead of a disheartened spirit. (Isaiah 61:3)

Seeing the best in any situation and keeping a positive outlook is possible only because of the promises found in God's Word. In Romans 8:28, the apostle Paul says: "And we know that in all things God works for the good of those who love him, who have been called according to his purpose" (NIV).

Notice that verse doesn't say God works *some* things together for your good; it says *all* things. Every situation, every encounter, every trial, every challenge—God is going to work it out for your good.

God can take the most difficult things you've been through and use them for your benefit. He will give you "beauty for ashes" and "the oil of joy for mourning" (Isaiah 61:3 NKJV). God didn't cause the pain or the dysfunction you've suffered, but He can heal your wounds and use what you've been through to accomplish something beautiful.

Today's Thought

Whatever you may be going through right now, believe and say, "God will work this out for my good!"

Dig Deeper into God's Word: Study Psalm 86:5–7; Philippians 4:6–7

The Importance of God's Word

My son, attend to my words; incline thine ear unto my say-ings. (Proverbs 4:20 KJV)

The Bible is no ordinary book. The words within its pages are like medicine to your soul. It has the power to change your life, because there is life in the Word (see Hebrews 4:12). And when you discover the power and truth of God's Word, you will begin to see changes in your life that only this truth can bring.

Studying the Word of God is not complicated; you just have to begin and be determined to stick with it. Every time you spend time reading the Bible, pay attention to what you're reading, and you'll learn something that will benefit you.

Proverbs says, "My son, attend to my words." The word *attend* means you pay attention and give time to something. Attending to the Word of God means more than just reading it; it's about study-ing, meditating on it, and obeying what it says. Be diligent in Bible study, and what you learn will give you a life worth living.

Today's Thought

Anytime you need an encouraging word, you can find it in the Bible.

Dig Deeper into God's Word: Study James 1:22–25; 2 Timothy 3:16–17

How to Study God's Word

*Pay attention [and be willing to learn] so that you may gain
understanding and intelligent discernment. (Proverbs 4:1)*

Studying the Word of God is not a hard thing to do. Here are a few
ways you can begin today:

- Purposely set aside time. Make an appointment with God each
  day during a time that works best for you.
- Make preparation for your Bible study. Have a place where you
  enjoy being, somewhere you are comfortable, like a room in
  your house that is quiet.
- Have all your materials available. You'll want your Bible, a
  computer or notebook to write down what you learn, and perhaps a commentary on the book of the Bible you want to study.
- Prepare your heart. Talk to God about things you may need
  to confess, and enter your study time peacefully and without
  anything that may hinder you from focusing on Scripture and
  receiving revelation during your study time.

  This is not an exhaustive list, but it's a great way to get started
studying God's Word and growing deeper in your relationship
with Him.

Today's Thought

The most important time you spend is your time with God.

Dig Deeper into God's Word: Study Proverbs 18:15;
    Proverbs 1:5

Are You Available?

Then I heard the voice of the Lord, saying, "Whom shall I send, and who will go for Us?" Then I said, "Here am I. Send me!" (Isaiah 6:8)

Many times we focus on our weaknesses, concerned that they will somehow disqualify us from doing something for God. But you don't have to be worried about your weaknesses, because they do not surprise God. He already knows everything there is to know about you, and He will use you in spite of your perceived weakness.

God is not looking for our *ability*; He's looking for our *availability*.

Instead of waking up each morning thinking about what you can't do, take some time with the Lord and say, *Here I am, God. Is there anything You want me to do today? Do You have an assignment for me? I'm going to be confident and bold in Your strength, Lord. I'm available for whatever You have planned for me.*

If you have an open heart and an available spirit, you'll be amazed at the ways God will use you to help and bless people.

Today's Thought

It's not your natural gift, ability, or strength that impresses God. He is looking for those whose hearts are fully committed to Him (see 2 Chronicles 16:9).

Dig Deeper into God's Word: Study 2 Corinthians
    12:9; Exodus 3:11–12

The Healing Power of Truth

Behold, You desire truth in the innermost being, and in the hidden part [of my heart] You will make me know wisdom. (Psalm 51:6)

God's Word is truth, and when we love it and obey it, we are set free from bondages that have held us captive. Don't ever be afraid of truth. It brings light into your life and dispels darkness.

Anything we hide has authority over us, but the moment we bring it out into the light, it is exposed and loses its power. We instantly feel that a huge burden has lifted, and our lives are made better. This is the freeing power of living in truth.

The Holy Spirit is given to us after we receive Jesus as our Savior, so He can consistently teach us and reveal truth to us. It is an ongoing process in our lives and one that can and should be exciting.

Today's Thought

What has God been trying to reveal to you? Have you been hiding in the dark? If so, I urge you to come out into the light and begin your journey of total healing.

Dig Deeper into God's Word: Study John 8:32;
    John 17:17

Separating Your "Who" from Your "Do"

For Christ is the end of the law [it leads to Him and its purpose is fulfilled in Him], for [granting] righteousness to everyone who believes [in Him as Savior]. (Romans 10:4)

Sometimes we have the tendency to make things complicated. We may fall into trying to please God or win His love by doing good works or working our way into right standing with Him. But our relationship with God is not based on what we do but on what Jesus did for us and whether we accept it.

Our motivation is very important to God. He wants us to do what we do for Him out of a heart of love and sincere desire. He does not want us to do things to get something from Him or to impress people.

We can be assured that God loves us, even on the days we don't do everything perfectly. God doesn't love us because of what we do, but because of who we are in Christ. In other words, it is important to know how to separate our "who" from our "do."

Today's Thought

You won't always do everything right, but you are still in right standing before God because of the finished work of Christ Jesus.

Dig Deeper into God's Word: Study Colossians 3:23; 1 Corinthians 15:58

Look Up

I will lift up my eyes to the hills—from whence comes my help? My help comes from the Lord, who made heaven and earth. (Psalm 121:1–2 NKJV)

A lot of people look to the wrong things when they find themselves in difficult situations. They focus on the size of their problem, the risks that they're facing, the negative things others are saying about them, or their fear of failure. Those things drag them down, and looking to them will not help them.

The Word of God gives us a much better option when we're in need of help. Instead of looking down at the things that can't help us, the Bible tells us to look up—to put our focus on the One who will always help us. When David was in trouble, he would turn and cast his eyes upward, because he knew his help came from on high.

When you're going through something and not sure what to do, use your spiritual eyes and just look up. Look for the Lord. He is the One who can help you. He is the One who will rescue you.

Today's Thought

Jesus said to look up, for our redemption draws near (see Luke 21:28). This is talking about more than a physical posture. This is having a hopeful attitude, a positive outlook, and an expectation that God will bring you through.

Dig Deeper into God's Word: Study 1 Chronicles 16:11; Psalm 34:10

Success Requires Effort

The thief comes only in order to steal and kill and destroy.
I came that they may have and enjoy life, and have it in
abundance [to the full, till it overflows]. (John 10:10)

True success does not come easily or without hurdles for anyone. It is the result of hard work, patience, sacrifice, and determination—but it does come. As a child of God, the only way you will ever be a failure is if you give up.

You can be successful in every area of your life—work, relationships, marriage, pursuit of God's plans, and everything else in which you are involved. But lasting success requires effort, and as you work toward it, the enemy will try to oppose you.

It's crucial to learn to keep moving forward in God's strength when success does not come as easily as you would like. When you face the obstacles that you are sure to encounter along the way, don't give up. Keep moving forward with determination!

Today's Thought

When you are tempted to give up, that's when you need to get up and keep being diligent.

Dig Deeper into God's Word: Study Proverbs 16:3;
     Ecclesiastes 9:10

Releasing Your Faith

God has apportioned to each a degree of faith [and a pur-pose designed for service]. (Romans 12:3)

Faith is something that must be released. You can possess faith, but it doesn't do you any good if you don't put it to use. A muscle that is not used gets weak and shrivels up. It's the same way with your faith: If you don't use it, then it's no different from not having any.

When you sit down in a chair, you have faith that it's not going to collapse. You don't start sweating and trembling with fear, say-ing, "Oh, I'm afraid to sit in this chair. I don't know if I should be doing this!" Your faith in the chair allows you to rest in it.

But what about when you have a problem? Do you put your faith in Jesus and rest in Him? Surely we can trust Him much more than we do a chair!

In your quiet time with God today, release your faith through prayer, and be ready to do whatever He asks you to do. Wait patiently on Him and don't worry.

Today's Thought

Worry doesn't help God solve our problems, but it does make us miserable. Choose to trust God and put your faith to work!

Dig Deeper into God's Word: Study Matthew 17:20;
    Romans 1:17

Jesus Holds All Things Together

And He Himself existed and is before all things, and in Him all things hold together. [His is the controlling, cohesive force of the universe.] (Colossians 1:17)

This is a powerful scripture. It tells us Jesus is holding *everything* together. Think about it. We can't have good relationships if Jesus isn't holding them together. Our finances and everything else would be a mess without Jesus. But if He is capable of holding the entire universe together, surely we can trust Him to hold us together, too.

Matthew 6:33 tells us to seek God and His kingdom first. If we don't have first things first, everything else will be out of balance. So make Jesus the most important thing in your life. Start today by giving Him first place in everything you do. He's holding you and everything that concerns you together.

Today's Thought

We always find time to do what is important to us, and if God is first, then finding time for Him won't be difficult.

Dig Deeper Into God's Word· Study Hebrews 1:1-3; John 1:3

Your Strong Shelter

He who dwells in the shelter of the Most High will remain secure and rest in the shadow of the Almighty [whose power no enemy can withstand]. (Psalm 91:1)

We all face storms in life sometimes. If you think about it, the best way to be safe during a natural storm is to take cover. If you do not seek shelter, the storm may harm you. Well, the same thing is true spiritually.

The Word of God gives us instructions on how to take cover when we face the spiritual storms of life. The first place you need to run to when a storm hits in your life is the secret place of the Most High, the presence of God.

The secret place of the Most High is His presence, and we enter it by faith when we spend time with Him. As you regularly study God's Word and invite Him into all areas of your life, you are developing spiritual disciplines that are stronger than any storm you may encounter. When you practice these habits, you actually construct spiritual walls of protection around yourself in Christ.

Today's Thought

Don't worry or become afraid when dealing with the storms of life. Jesus is with you, and He will speak to your storm and cause the winds and the waves to become calm at just the right time.

Dig Deeper into God's Word: Study Psalm 46:1–5; Psalm 61:4

Laugh on Purpose

*Restore to me the joy of Your salvation and sustain me with
a willing spirit. (Psalm 51:12)*

One of the most valuable things I have learned in my life is that I
don't have to wait to *feel* like doing something before I can do it...and
neither do you. You can actually create opportunities for laughter.

- *Plan to laugh...and then do it.* Take a few minutes away from
  the busyness of the day and focus on something funny that a
  friend said or something enjoyable you're looking forward to.
- *Hang around funny and encouraging people.* Spend time with
  people who are lighthearted and encouraging. Their humor
  and their positive nature are infectious.
- *Change your perspective.* You can be joyful if you begin each
  day with a think session. Think about some happy, joyful
  things on purpose.

Learn to enjoy yourself rather than being so intense about your
imperfections. I can promise it will add laughter to your life.

David prayed, "Restore to me the joy of Your salvation." We
can pray the same thing. If you feel life has sapped you of your joy
and taken away your laughter, ask God for His help and take every
opportunity you can to laugh.

Today's Thought

*Laughter relieves stress and helps promote healing in our
body.*

Dig Deeper into God's Word: Study Job 8:21;
Psalm 126:2

When God's Passion Becomes Your Passion

And if you offer yourself to [assist] the hungry and satisfy the need of the afflicted, then your light will rise in darkness and your gloom will become like midday. (Isaiah 58:10)

God is passionate about helping people who are hurting and in need. The closer you get to God and the more your love for Him grows, the more determined you become to live each day in a way that will make someone else's life better. God's passion becomes your passion.

Helping people should be a top priority of living the Christian life. Jesus always went about doing good (see Acts 10:38).

If you reach beyond your own situation and bring Christ's love to others, your peace and joy will increase, making the struggles you face seem to fade away. And you'll experience the amazing satisfaction of making a difference where it counts.

Today's Thought

Selfish people are never happy people, so get busy helping others, and your joy will increase.

Dig Deeper into God's Word: Study James 1:27; Romans 12:10

Trading Worry for Peace

Cast your burden on the Lord [release it] and He will sus-tain and uphold you, He will never allow the righteous to be shaken (slip, fall, fail). (Psalm 55:22)

God wants to make a trade with you today. He wants you to give Him all your cares, problems, and failures. In exchange, He'll give you His peace and contentment.

God really does want to take care of us, but in order for that to happen, we need to stop trying to fix everything ourselves and worrying about every problem we encounter. Sometimes we want God to take care of us, but instead of trusting, we fret and try to find ways to help ourselves through reasoning.

God will give you His peace, but first you must give Him your worry. What a fantastic trade! You can give God all your cares and concerns, and then trust that your answer is on the way.

Today's Thought

You don't have to have all the answers... and that's okay! God knows the end from the beginning, and He already has it all figured out. Trust Him and make the trade today.

Dig Deeper into God's Word: Study 1 Peter 5:6–7;
    Isaiah 26:3

The Opinions of Others

*For whoever comes [near] to God must [necessarily] believe
that God exists and that He rewards those who [earnestly
and diligently] seek Him. (Hebrews 11:6)*

One of the things we often must give up in order to serve God with
our whole hearts is our reputation. There are those who will not be
supportive of your walk with God, and you have to learn not to let
their opinions hold you back.

Jesus "made Himself of no reputation" (see Philippians 2:7 NKJV),
and it is easy now for me to understand why. If we care too much
about what people think of us, we will never fully follow Christ. I
sacrificed my reputation with the people I knew at the time God
called me, and now He has rewarded me. I have many more friends
now than those I gave up long ago.

If you are suffering the loss of your reputation or being unfairly
judged and criticized because of your faith in God, don't despair.
Continue seeking God in your quiet time with Him, and look forward to your reward.

Today's Thought

*God rewards those who diligently seek Him. When you are
suffering persecution, look forward to the reward God has
planned for you.*

Dig Deeper into God's Word: Study 1 Thessalonians
4:1; Galatians 1:10

The Basis for Your Hope

For the word of the Lord is right; and all His work is done in faithfulness. (Psalm 33:4)

Hope needs to have a platform to stand on. We need a reason to hope, and David said that his reason was the Word of God. David simply put his trust in God's faithfulness to fulfill His Word.

Why is the study and meditation of God's Word so important? It is seed, and seed always produces after its own kind. The more you study the promises of God, the more hopeful you will be.

I strongly urge you to read, study, listen to, and meditate on God's Word as often as possible with a believing heart. When we plant the seed of God's Word in our hearts, it brings a harvest of many good things.

Put your hope in God and His Word! When we live with hope, we can see deliverance from our problems, and we can enjoy our life in Christ Jesus.

Today's Thought

Hope is a positive expectation that something good is going to happen.

Dig Deeper into God's Word: Study Mark 4:24–25;
    Romans 15:4

The Best Way to Pray

Father, if You are willing, remove this cup [of divine wrath] from Me; yet not My will, but [always] Yours be done. (Luke 22:42)

Let me suggest the best way for you to pray. Instead of merely telling God what you want Him to do for you, try asking for what you want but then adding this statement: *But, Lord, if this isn't the right thing for me, then please don't give it to me!*

Getting our own way is highly overrated. It is amazing how much of our lives is wasted on the pursuit of self-gratification, only to find in the end that we are not satisfied at all. This is what happens when we trust ourselves instead of trusting God.

Only God's will has the ability to ultimately satisfy us. We are created for Him and His purposes, and anything less than that is totally incapable of bringing lasting contentment. God knows what is best for your life, and there is no better place to be than in the middle of His perfect will.

Today's Thought

Trust God to give you His best for you, rather than just what you want.

Dig Deeper into God's Word: Study Proverbs 19:21; Matthew 6:10

The Higher You Go,
the Clearer You See

*From the end of the earth I call to You, when my heart is
overwhelmed and weak; lead me to the rock that is higher
than I [a rock that is too high to reach without Your help].
(Psalm 61:2)*

When hikers get lost and they're trying to figure out exactly where
they are, they look to go higher. A higher vantage point gives them
a better perspective.

The same is true for us. Sometimes it's hard to see where we're
going because we have limited vision. We can become confused by
our problems and unsure where to go next because we don't have
the right perspective. In order to get God's perspective, spend your
quiet time with Him going higher.

Hike past ingratitude; climb above doubt and discouragement.
If you choose higher expectations and higher hopes, you'll begin
to get a new perspective—a godly perspective. And when that happens, you're going to be able to see God's plan for your life clearer
than you ever have before.

Today's Thought

*Don't focus on your problems; choose to climb higher and
rise above them with God's help.*

Dig Deeper into God's Word: Study Isaiah 55:8–9;
    Colossians 3:2

Rejecting Offense

Good sense and discretion make a man slow to anger, and it is his honor and glory to overlook a transgression or an offense [without seeking revenge and harboring resentment]. (Proverbs 19:11)

There is a test we all have to pass in life, and I call it the "get over being offended" test. This can also be called the bitterness-resentment-and-unforgiveness test. The only way to get over being offended is to forgive. The sooner you do it, the easier it will be.

Don't let offense take root in your heart, because it will be more difficult to deal with if you do.

One of our first responses when someone hurts or offends us should be to pray: *God, I choose to believe the best. My feelings are hurt, but You can heal me. I refuse to be bitter; I refuse to be angry or to stay offended.*

Don't let someone else's behavior frustrate your day or ruin your life. Take the high road and forgive.

Today's Thought

When you forgive, you are actually doing yourself a favor. You are freeing yourself from the agony of anger and bitter thoughts.

Dig Deeper into God's Word: Study Matthew 18:7;
  Psalm 139:23-24

God Is Greater

Little children (believers, dear ones), you are of God and you belong to Him and have [already] overcome them [the agents of the antichrist]; because He who is in you is greater than he (Satan) who is in the world [of sinful mankind]. (1 John 4:4)

The Word of God tells us that we do have an enemy: Satan. And though we should be aware of his schemes, let me be clear: You have nothing to fear. The devil has no real power over the children of God—none!

The moment you gave your life to the Lord, you became a redeemed, forgiven, righteous child of God. Satan has no rightful place in your life. You have the presence of God in your life. He is your strength, and He promises you victory.

Rather than live in fear of your enemy, trust that you are empowered by God to live a bold, confident, productive, happy life that overcomes the enemy at every turn. You never have to live in worry or fear, wondering if you are going to be defeated.

Live with the assurance that greater is He who is in you than he who is in the world.

Today's Thought

The enemy may come against you, but God is on your side, so your victory is a sure thing.

Dig Deeper into God's Word: Study Luke 10:19; Revelation 17:14

Ask Boldly

For this reason I am telling you, whatever things you ask for in prayer [in accordance with God's will], believe [with confident trust] that you have received them, and they will be given to you. (Mark 11:24)

One of the benefits of being a child of God is that we can ask Him for the things we need or want in life. Sometimes people are reluctant to ask boldly for big things, but Jesus has given us permission to step out in faith and ask boldly.

Don't waste precious time wondering. Some people wonder what it would be like if God would give them a better job. They wonder what it would be like to own their own home or have a baby. They wish they had healthier relationships, could overcome a bad habit or debilitating fear, or were in better physical health. Don't wonder—ask!

Wondering and indecision can become strongholds in our minds that can leave us feeling confused, insecure, and ineffective. But that's not God's plan. He wants us to overcome the wondering thoughts by believing and then receiving the answer to our prayers from God, by faith.

Today's Thought

Faith gives us the confidence to ask boldly, knowing that God will answer our prayers in the way that is best. He has a great plan for your life. Don't hesitate to ask boldly when you pray.

Dig Deeper into God's Word: Study Matthew 7:7;
    James 4:2

Embrace the New You

And we all, with unveiled face, continually seeing as in a mirror the glory of the Lord, are progressively being transformed into His image from [one degree of] glory to [even more] glory, which comes from the Lord, [who is] the Spirit. (2 Corinthians 3:18)

We all enter our relationship with God with many things about us that need to change. We cannot change ourselves by mere willpower, but God does change us. It is a process that takes time, and because of that we often think that nothing is changing, but it is. Don't look at how far you still have to go; look at how far you have come.

God changes us from the inside out. Our part is to trust Him and believe that He has made us new creatures in Him as His Word says (see 2 Corinthians 5:17).

The more we renew our mind by studying God's Word, the more we will live in the reality of His promise. Start to see yourself the way God sees you, and above all be patient and always believe that God is working, even if you can't see what He is doing.

Today's Thought

As long as you continue believing, God continues working!

Dig Deeper into God's Word: Study Philippians 2:13;
     Ephesians 4:24

Who You Are in Christ

I have been crucified with Christ [that is, in Him I have shared His crucifixion]; it is no longer I who live, but Christ lives in me. (Galatians 2:20)

Sometimes we forget who we really are in Christ Jesus. We look to other things to find our identity, but when we accept Jesus as our Savior, our identity is wrapped up in Him. Here are just a few of the things the Word of God says that you are:

- You are the righteousness of God—you have right standing with Him—in Jesus Christ (see 2 Corinthians 5:21).
- You are born of God and belong to Him, therefore, the enemy cannot touch you (see 1 John 5:18).
- You are saved by God's grace, alive in Christ, and have everything Jesus died to give you (see Ephesians 2:5–6; Colossians 2:12).
- You are more than a conqueror through Christ, who loves you (see Romans 8:37).
- You are the head and not the tail; you only go up in life, not down, as you trust and obey God (see Deuteronomy 28:13).
- You are a new creation in Christ (see 2 Corinthians 5:17).

You are not a failure or a mistake. God has a plan and a purpose for you, and many good things await you in your future.

Today's Thought

You have been given a powerful new identity in Christ. Don't let the devil tell you that you are anything less than who you are.

Dig Deeper into God's Word: Study Ephesians 1:4; Hebrews 10:39

Fearfully and Wonderfully Made

I will give thanks and praise to You, for I am fearfully and
wonderfully made; wonderful are Your works, and my soul
knows it very well. (Psalm 139:14)

Insecurities are often born from hurtful things others have said
about you or lies the enemy tells you, but they grow only when you
decide to nurture them. As a child of God, you don't have to live
under the storm clouds of insecurity.

When you choose to believe that you are accepted and loved by
God, you will never need to be insecure around people again.

God wants you to live with a bold confidence, believing in
faith that His plans and purposes will come to pass in your life.
Good things don't happen in our lives because we deserve them,
but because God is good and He loves us. Believe by faith that all
things are possible with God—including all of the great things He
wants to do for you and through you.

Today's Thought

God loves me unconditionally, and He's always working in
my life. I'm okay and I'm on my way!

Dig Deeper into God's Word: Study Hebrews 4:16;
    Philippians 1:6

Saying No to a Complaining Attitude

Do everything without murmuring or questioning [the providence of God]. (Philippians 2:14)

One of the biggest traps we fall into as Christians is the trap of grumbling and complaining, which seems to be an ever-present temptation in our lives. It's so natural to complain that it seems that we are born with a complaining attitude—we don't have to develop one.

On the other hand, we do have to develop and nurture a thankful attitude. This is a choice we can make each day in our quiet time with God. If we make it a priority to stay busy praising, worshipping, and thanking God, there will be no room for complaining, faultfinding, or murmuring.

Complaining does nothing but ruin what could be a good day, and it leaves us feeling unhappy, but thankfulness does the opposite. A grateful heart reminds us of how blessed we are and how good God is to us all the time.

Today's Thought

Each time you are tempted to complain, pray instead.

Dig Deeper into God's Word: Study 1 Peter 4:9; James 5:9

Even If You're the Only One

All these blessings will come upon you and overtake you if you pay attention to the voice of the Lord your God. (Deuteronomy 28:2)

When we do God's will, His presence is with us and we are sure to succeed. But when we fail to follow Him, we invite all kinds of problems into our lives. Are you willing to say yes to God, even if it means saying no to your friends or even to yourself?

We can choose to be people who want to obey God and follow Him more than anything else. We can be strong and courageous and do whatever God leads us to do.

Even if you are the only person you know who is doing the right thing, I encourage you to obey God. Do not follow your flesh, your friends, or your own wishes. When we follow God, He always leads us to good things.

Today's Thought

Being obedient to God always increases your peace.

Dig Deeper into God's Word: Study Acts 5:29;
     Isaiah 1:19

Just as You Are

*But to as many as did receive and welcome Him, He gave
the right [the authority, the privilege] to become children
of God, that is, to those who believe in (adhere to, trust in,
and rely on) His name. (John 1:12)*

Sometimes we think we must improve before we can have a relationship with God, but grace meets us where we are in our imperfect state and makes us what God wants us to be. Grace finds us
where we are, but it never leaves us where it found us.

Grace takes us the way we are. I like to say that when God invites
us to His party, it is always a "come as you are" party.

Don't waste years of your life trying to improve before you enter
into relationship with God. Come as you are!

Today's Thought

When you make mistakes, don't run from God—run to Him!

Dig Deeper into God's Word: Study Romans 5:8;
    Romans 8:29

Joy Is a Gift from God

Rejoice in the Lord always [delight, take pleasure in Him];
again I will say, rejoice! (Philippians 4:4)

When we receive Jesus into our lives as our Savior, we receive all
that He is in our spirit. We receive the Holy Spirit and all the fruit
of the Spirit, including the fruit of joy.

The first step in accessing the gifts God has given you through
your faith in Christ is to believe that you have them. Sad Christians
are people who simply don't know what they have in Christ. They
don't know what He has done for them.

Joy is a calm delight we can have all the time, regardless of our
circumstances. It is a gift from God. And Jesus died that we might
have and enjoy our lives in abundance and to the full (see John
10:10).

Today's Thought

Jesus gave His life so you can have His righteousness,
peace, and joy in your life every day.

Dig Deeper into God's Word: Study 1 Peter 1:8;
John 15:11

One Day at a Time

Give us this day our daily bread. (Matthew 6:11)

God helps us as we put our trust in Him, not as we worry and fret about how we are going to solve our future problems. When we use today to worry about tomorrow, we end up wasting today. It is useless. Instead, we can come to God, trusting His provision, one day at a time.

Our walk with God is called a "daily walk" for a reason: We need His help every day.

We can get out of debt, exercise, lose weight, graduate from college, parent a special needs child, or be successful at anything we need to do if we will put our trust in God and take life one day at a time. Jesus said not to worry about tomorrow, because tomorrow would have sufficient trouble of its own (see Matthew 6:34).

Today's Thought

Walk in faith, and God's grace will meet you every step of the way.

Dig Deeper into God's Word: Study Matthew 6:34;
   Romans 1:17

Living Consecrated to God

He chose us in Christ [actually selected us for Himself as His own] before the foundation of the world, so that we would be holy [that is, consecrated, set apart for Him, purpose-driven] and blameless in His sight. (Ephesians 1:4)

Doing everything as unto the Lord with all of your heart is one mark of a consecrated life. It is one way we can say, "God, I belong to You." Consecration brings blessing. It is an honor to give your life to the Lord.

The apostle Paul wrote, "Do you not know that your body is a temple of the Holy Spirit who is within you, whom you have [received as a gift] from God, and that you are not your own [property]? You were bought with a price [you were actually purchased with the precious blood of Jesus and made His own]. So then, honor and glorify God with your body" (1 Corinthians 6:19–20).

We have been bought with a price—the blood of Jesus Christ. God purchased us for Himself. We no longer belong to ourselves; we belong to God, and our daily goal should be to follow and serve Him in all things.

Saying yes to God often requires us to say no to ourselves, but as we do, our joy and peace are multiplied.

Today's Thought

Whatever you do today, do it for the Lord because you love Him and want to please Him.

Dig Deeper into God's Word: Study Mark 8:34; Psalm 100:3

Pray Your Way through Every Day

*With all prayer and petition pray [with specific requests]
at all times [on every occasion and in every season] in the
Spirit, and with this in view, stay alert with all perseverance and petition [interceding in prayer] for all God's people. (Ephesians 6:18)*

God wants us to enjoy set-apart times of prayer, but that is not the
only way to pray. He longs for us to pray simple prayers to Him on a
continual basis. He wants us to live a life of prayer and to pray our
way through every day. His desire is for our hearts to be sensitive
to the many things He does for us and to remember to whisper,
"Thank You, Lord!"

God is eager for us to ask Him for everything we need in every
situation and to enjoy conversation with Him as we go about the
activities of our lives. He is ever-present, and you can talk to Him
about anything at any time.

Today's Thought

*Prayer opens the door for God to work in every area of
your life.*

Dig Deeper into God's Word: Study Psalm 66:19;
    Luke 6:12

How to Win in Life

And do not be conformed to this world [any longer with its superficial values and customs], but be transformed and progressively changed [as you mature spiritually] by the renewing of your mind [focusing on godly values and ethical attitudes]. (Romans 12:2)

Nobody is successful in any venture by just wishing they would be. Successful people make a plan and keep it before them, in their minds, consistently. You can choose what you think about and dwell on.

We are in a war, and the mind is the battlefield. But as Romans 12:2 says, we are transformed to become more like Christ as we renew our minds with God's truth.

If you have had years of experiencing wrong thinking and letting your emotions lead you, making the change may not be easy, but the results will be worth it. In your quiet time with God, choose what you are going to think about. Focus on God's promises and your identity in Christ. With God's guidance, make a plan of how you are going to be successful in fulfilling all He has for you to do today, and then keep that plan at the forefront of your mind.

Today's Thought

Learn to think according to the Word of God, and your emotions and actions will start lining up with your thoughts.

Dig Deeper into God's Word: Study Ephesians 4:22–24; 1 Peter 5:8

Progressive Knowledge

But I tell you the truth, it is to your advantage that I go away; for if I do not go away, the Helper (Comforter, Advocate, Intercessor—Counselor, Strengthener, Standby) will not come to you; but if I go, I will send Him (the Holy Spirit) to you [to be in close fellowship with you]. (John 16:7)

Knowledge is progressive, and we don't learn everything we need to know overnight. Jesus told His disciples He still had many things to say to them, but they would not be able to grasp everything then. Jesus was going away, but the Father would send the Spirit of Truth to guide them and teach them all things.

It is wonderful to know that we have the Holy Spirit to guide us through life, and that He will never leave us. He leads us into truth and the truth makes us free (see John 8:32).

The Holy Spirit advises us and empowers us to live the life God desires for us one day at a time. Learn to follow Him because He will always lead you to the right place at the right time.

Today's Thought

You are never alone! God's Spirit is with you, and He is for you.

Dig Deeper into God's Word: Study John 14:26; 2 Corinthians 3:18

His Word Abides in You

If you abide in Me, and My words abide in you, you will ask what you desire, and it shall be done for you. (John 15:7 NKJV)

To abide in God's Word means to live, dwell, and remain in it. Keep it in the center of your heart and let it be your guide through life. I firmly believe that we find every answer we need for life in God's Word.

God is not someone that we visit for one hour on Sunday morning, but He is our life. We need Him every moment of every day. Jesus is the Word, so when we abide in the Word, we abide in Him.

Abiding in the Word and allowing the Word to abide in you adds power to your life. It adds power in prayer, power over the enemy, and power to keep pressing toward the will of God for your life.

Make a decision today to begin studying God's Word. If you dedicate some time each day, before long you will find that you have learned many things that are helping you in your daily life.

Today's Thought

Don't try to work time with God into your schedule, but work your schedule around Him, and things will go much better.

Dig Deeper into God's Word: Study Matthew 4:4; John 8:31–32

Facing Your Problems

When the righteous cry [for help], the Lord hears and rescues them from all their distress and troubles. (Psalm 34:17)

Because the world we live in is broken and full of sin, we will face problems as we walk through life. But don't be discouraged; Jesus gave us a great promise. He said that when we face troubles in life we can "be courageous [be confident, be undaunted, be filled with joy]," for He has overcome the world (John 16:33).

You don't have to focus on your problem. Focus on Jesus—He has overcome your problem!

The battle has already been won, and all we need to do is take steps of faith and obedience, realizing that each step is leading us closer and closer to experiencing the victory that is already ours in Christ. Whatever problem you are up against today, take a new approach: Instead of comparing that obstacle to *your* ability, compare that obstacle to *God's* ability.

Today's Thought

Your problem may seem bigger than you are, but it's not bigger than God.

Dig Deeper into God's Word: Study Psalm 57:2;
    Isaiah 58:8

Freedom for the Taking

And you will know the truth [regarding salvation], and the truth will set you free [from the penalty of sin]. (John 8:32)

John 8:32 says that when we know God's Word and follow it, it will make us free. There may be things you want to be free from, but there are also things you may want to be free to do.

In Christ, we're free to step out with confidence and try something new. Making mistakes is often how we learn, so don't be afraid to try.

In Christ, you're also free to enjoy life, to enjoy God, and to enjoy yourself. Jesus didn't die for us so we could be miserable; He came that we might have and enjoy our lives (see John 10:10).

Today's Thought

You don't have to live in bondage to fear, doubt, or insecurity. You are a redeemed, forgiven, empowered child of God. Live in confidence and security in God's love for you today—you are free!

Dig Deeper into God's Word: Study Galatians 5:1; 2 Corinthians 3:17

To Know Him More

But from there you will seek the Lord your God, and you
will find Him if you search for Him with all your heart and
all your soul. (Deuteronomy 4:29)

Determination is required if we want anything good in life...
including a deeper relationship with God.

The apostle Paul didn't want to merely know *about* God; he
was determined to know *Him* personally (see Philippians 3:10).
He wanted to have an intimate, personal relationship with Him.
This is available to anyone who desires it and is willing to seek God
wholeheartedly.

There is so much more to learn about how amazing God is, and
we will know more as we seek Him more. As we make our journey
in life with Him, we find that He is with us in all kinds of situations. He never leaves us or forsakes us. And when we have experienced God's power in our lives, it becomes easier to trust Him the
next time we have a need.

Today's Thought

Don't ever be satisfied with knowing about God—be deter-
mined to know Him personally and intimately.

Dig Deeper into God's Word: Study Psalm 46:10;
   Ephesians 3:17–19

Pitiful or Powerful

When Jesus noticed him lying there [helpless], knowing that he had been in that condition a long time, He said to him, "Do you want to get well?... Get up; pick up your pallet and walk." (John 5:6, 8)

For many years, I gave in to self-pity. "Why me, God?" was the question that dominated my thoughts and determined my outlook. I felt as though I was owed something because of the way I had been mistreated as a child, but instead of looking to God for help, I was simply stuck feeling sorry for myself.

Isn't it interesting that when Jesus met the man who had been lying by the pool of Bethesda for thirty-eight years waiting for a miracle, He asked if he was serious about getting well? Many people would like a miracle, but like the man in our story, they are not willing to give up their blame and self-pity.

God wants to give us beauty for ashes, but it is essential that we be willing to let go of the ashes. That means we must give up the self-pity, blame, and bitter attitudes. Today can be a new beginning for you if you are willing to let go of the past and trust God to fully restore your life.

Today's Thought

You can be pitiful or powerful... but you can't be both.

Dig Deeper into God's Word: Study Isaiah 61:1–3;
       Ephesians 6:10

Letting Go of Bitterness

Let all bitterness and wrath and anger and clamor [perpetual animosity, resentment, strife, fault-finding] and slander be put away from you, along with every kind of malice [all spitefulness, verbal abuse, malevolence]. (Ephesians 4:31)

Unresolved bitterness is an anchor that doesn't just hold you back, it drags you down. It causes you to stay in the past, reliving the hurt you experienced every day, pulling you further and further away from God. The longer you hold on to past abuse, betrayal, rejection, or injustice, the further you'll be from your destiny.

Forgiveness is a choice. It doesn't happen accidentally. You must decide that you are going to resist the devil's attempts to keep you living in the pain of the past and then depend on the power of the Holy Spirit to help you be obedient to God's Word. When you make the choice to let go of bitterness and forgive, it's like waking up to a brand-new life!

Today's Thought

You'll be amazed at how much better you'll feel—physically, emotionally, and spiritually—when you choose to let go of bitterness and unforgiveness.

Dig Deeper into God's Word: Study Hebrews 12:15; 2 Timothy 2:24

The Fruit of Self-Control

Like a city that is broken down and without walls [leaving it unprotected] is a man who has no self-control over his spirit [and sets himself up for trouble]. (Proverbs 25.28)

People often say that they have no self-control, but if they are Christians, that is not accurate. God has given us the power and ability to control our thoughts, words, and actions. We are not to try to control other people, and we cannot control all of the circumstances in our lives, but we can control ourselves.

Self-control is actually a fruit of the Spirit-led life (see Galatians 5:22–23). If you have a tendency to want to control the people and circumstances in your life, ask God to help you control yourself instead. The more we exercise self-control, the easier it will become to do it.

When a circumstance is unpleasant or even downright painful, exercise self-control. Pray right away, asking God to help you control yourself and have a godly response to the situation rather than an emotional one.

Today's Thought

Although we cannot always control how we feel, we can control how we behave.

Dig Deeper into God's Word: Study 2 Peter 1:5–7;
    Ecclesiastes 7:9

What Are You Hoping For?

Return to the stronghold, you prisoners of hope. Even today I declare that I will restore double to you. (Zechariah 9:12 NKJV)

What are you hoping for today? What are you expecting in life? Are you looking for something good to happen, or are you expecting to be disappointed?

So many people are feeling hopeless these days. However, Jesus did not die for us to be hopeless. He died so that we could be full of hope.

The devil wants to steal your hope, and he will lie to you in order to do that. He will tell you that nothing good can happen in your life or that the good things you care about won't last. But stay full of hope, and remember that the devil is a liar. God's Word is truth, and His promises bring hope.

Our Father is good, and He has good plans for you. So refuse to give up hope and instead become a prisoner of hope! Start expecting God to do something wonderful in your life.

Today's Thought

If you maintain your hope, especially in the midst of troubled and uncertain times, God has promised you double for your trouble.

Dig Deeper into God's Word: Study Isaiah 61:7; Proverbs 23:18

No More Shame

For the Lord God helps Me, therefore, I have not been
ashamed or humiliated. Therefore, I have made My face like
flint, and I know that I shall not be put to shame. (Isaiah 50:7)

It is one thing to be ashamed of something you have done wrong,
but it is another thing entirely to become ashamed of yourself.
Shame is actually much deeper and more damaging than guilt.

If this is a problem for you, I have wonderful news: Jesus has
taken away the reproach of sin (the guilt *and* shame)! He bore it all.
He has declared you not guilty and made you a brand-new creation
in Him (see 2 Corinthians 5:17).

When you feel condemned, it is not Jesus condemning you; it is
the devil, and you must resist him. When you are having a guilt-
and-shame attack, just remember who you are in Christ. I recommend saying out loud, "God loves me unconditionally, and He has
forgiven all of my sins."

Today's Thought

God wants you to love and accept yourself.

Dig Deeper into God's Word: Study Romans 8:1–2;
   Psalm 119:6

No Pressure to Be Perfect

He hath made us accepted in the beloved. (Ephesians 1:6 KJV)

As we step out to be all we can be in Christ, we will make some mistakes—everyone does. But it takes the pressure off of us when we realize that God is not expecting us to be perfect, although He is delighted when that is our desire. Do your best each day, but don't live under the pressure of expecting yourself to do everything perfectly. If we could be perfect, then we would not need a Savior.

The world may demand perfection before it will accept us, but that is not what God demands. We can easily assume God is the way the world is, but He is not. The world will value you according to your performance, but God values you because you believe in His Beloved Son Jesus Christ.

Today's Thought

God knew every mistake you would ever make even before you were born, and He loves you anyway.

Dig Deeper into God's Word: Study Ephesians 2:8;
     Titus 2:11

A Step toward God

Come close to God [with a contrite heart] and He will come close to you. (James 4:8)

The Bible shows us that God took the first steps toward us—steps to building relationship with His children. When we were far from Him, lost in our own sin, God sent Jesus (see Romans 5:8). Stepping down from Heaven, walking perfectly on this earth, and going willingly to the cross, Jesus gave us what we could never earn in our own effort or strength—total forgiveness of sin, complete redemption, the chance to experience a personal relationship with God, and the promise of eternal life.

And now, through the precious gift of salvation, the Bible shows us that anytime we step toward God, He steps toward us again. And His steps are much bigger than ours.

In your quiet time with God, when you give Him your imperfect, flawed love, you receive His unconditional, perfect love in return. When you have faith as small as a mustard seed, God moves the mountains in your life. When you cast your cares on God, He gives you the peace that passes understanding. Just take a step and watch what God will do!

Today's Thought

You can trust God to come closer to you with each step you take toward Him.

Dig Deeper into God's Word: Study Psalm 73:28;
    Hebrews 7:25

Showing Real Love

*"Teacher, which is the greatest commandment in the Law?"
And Jesus replied to him, "'You shall love the Lord your
God with all your heart, and with all your soul, and with
all your mind.' This is the first and greatest commandment.
The second is like it, 'You shall love your neighbor as yourself [that is, unselfishly seek the best or higher good for oth-
ers].'" (Matthew 22:36–39)*

While every command from God is great and important, Jesus said
that the greatest or most important of all is that we walk in love.
We are to love God and love people as we love ourselves. He also
said that it is by this love that the world will know we are His disciples (see John 13:35).

Love is not just a theory or a teaching that inspires you; it is real
and practical. Love can be seen and felt, and it has miracle-working
power to change lives.

Walking in love will require us to make choices daily to live
beyond our emotions. We may not always "feel" like taking the
time to be kind to someone else, but each time we do, we are walking in love. Love is not a feeling we have but a choice we make
about how we will treat people.

Today's Thought

*Ask God to show you who you can help today, and He will
give you many opportunities.*

Dig Deeper into God's Word: Study 1 Corinthians 13:4;
    Luke 6:32

The Difference between Faith and Trust

Some trust in chariots and some in horses, but we will remember and trust in the name of the Lord our God. (Psalm 20:7)

The words *faith* and *trust* are often used interchangeably, but there is a difference. Faith is something we have, while trust is something we do.

God gives us faith. His Word says that every man is given a measure of faith (see Romans 12:3), but it is up to the individual what they do with it. Trust is faith in action. It is faith that has been released.

If you have not been doing so, make a decision to begin putting your trust in God in every situation in your life. In your time with God today, talk to Him about all the things you trust Him for. Trust God for your future, and trust Him for whatever challenging situation you are facing today. Trust Him to work in and through you to bring His will to pass.

Today's Thought

Out of all the things we put our trust in, God is the only source that is completely reliable.

Dig Deeper into God's Word: Study Psalm 13:5;
    Proverbs 3:5

The Power of Your Want-To

*Be devoted to one another with [authentic] brotherly affec-
tion...never lagging behind in diligence; aglow in the Spirit,
enthusiastically serving the Lord. (Romans 12:10–11)*

If you're determined and diligent, there is nothing or no one who
can stop you from obeying God and living the life He desires for
you to live. Make a decision to never give up and be determined to
outlast the devil, and eventually you will reach your goals.

We can do nothing without God, but neither does He do everything for us while we are passive and inactive. I have always
believed that if we do what we can do, God will do what we cannot do.

Your free will energized by God is one of the strongest forces on
earth. As you work together with Him, you will accomplish great
things.

Today's Thought

*Making the right choices today will help you enjoy tomor-
row more.*

Dig Deeper into God's Word: Study Proverbs 13:4;
    Philippians 2:13

New Things

*Listen carefully, I am about to do a new thing, now it will
spring forth; will you not be aware of it? (Isaiah 43:19)*

It's important to remember that God is on your side as you go into
new situations, because the enemy will always be lying in wait to
try to keep you from following the Holy Spirit. Satan's goal is to
make you so afraid that you decide not to walk into the new thing
God has for you.

Fear will call our attention to every possible negative thing
about a new situation and cause us to ignore all of the positives. To
focus on the positives, it is essential that you spend time with God
and look at the situation through eyes of faith.

Don't be afraid to step out and do something new. Perhaps
you haven't passed this way before, but God is with you, so press
through fear and opposition, and refuse to give up.

Today's Thought

*New opportunities and challenges are an exciting part of
your future. Don't let fear hold you back.*

Dig Deeper into God's Word: Study Deuteronomy 31:6;
    Psalm 27:1

The Dream in Your Heart

Hope deferred makes the heart sick, but a dream fulfilled is a tree of life. (Proverbs 13:12 NLT)

When God puts a dream in your heart, don't be afraid to pursue it. Dreams are different from plans. Plans are manageable opportunities, but dreams are often too big to be managed. You plan to assemble a model airplane, but you dream of flying.

Dreams will always require faith because they are bigger than our own ability to accomplish them. That is why faith-filled dreams are so important. When you dream a big dream for God, you become totally dependent on Him to bring it to pass.

If there is a dream in your heart, be diligent to seek God and obedient to take steps of faith to do anything He leads you to do. Plan on being patient, because dreams begin as seeds in our heart, and they take time and diligent care to be fulfilled.

Today's Thought

You will see your God-given dream come true in His timing if you do not give up.

Dig Deeper into God's Word: Study Psalm 20:4; Luke 1:45

Aware of Your Blessings

In everything give thanks; for this is the will of God in Christ Jesus for you. (1 Thessalonians 5:18 NKJV)

Giving thanks in everything means to be aware of the common, everyday blessings God gives us—our health, our freedom, a home to live in, family and friends, and many other blessings that we may easily take for granted.

We can also thank God all the time for the people that He puts in our lives. He gives us people to care for and support us, people to laugh with, people who challenge us, people to impart wisdom, and people with whom to enjoy life.

Being a thankful person adds tremendous benefits to your life. People enjoy being around someone who is thankful much more than someone who is a chronic complainer. Praying simple prayers of thanksgiving throughout the day is one of the best things you can do.

Today's Thought

When you spend time with God, ask for what you want and need, but don't forget to thank God for what you have.

Dig Deeper into God's Word: Study Psalm 107:1; Philippians 4:4

Adjust Your Sails

Constantly rejoicing in hope [because of our confidence in Christ], steadfast and patient in distress, devoted to prayer [continually seeking wisdom, guidance, and strength]. (Romans 12:12)

The world is filled with discouraged, downtrodden individuals who could make their situations better by simply choosing to put their hope in God.

Once we learn the power of hope and practice it, it is a hard habit to break. Just as people can form habits of being discouraged each time things don't go their way, we can learn to encourage ourselves through hoping and believing that a blessing is right around the corner.

What we say and do in difficult times determines how long the difficulty will last and how intense the difficulty will become. We cannot control everything that happens to us, but we can control how we respond to those things, and choosing the right words and actions helps us do that. You can't control the wind, but you can adjust the sails.

Today's Thought

Hope will motivate you to keep going when circumstances tell you to give up.

Dig Deeper into God's Word: Study Romans 8:5; Psalm 37:5

A Job Well Done

For God did not give us a spirit of timidity or cowardice or fear, but [He has given us a spirit] of power and of love and of sound judgment and personal discipline [abilities that result in a calm, well-balanced mind and self-control]. (2 Timothy 1:7)

Do you want to be happy and successful in life? If you do, then discipline is a must, and disciplining your emotions is especially important.

Many of our decisions are good, but if we don't follow through with them, they mean nothing. Excited emotions may help us get started in the right direction, but they are rarely there at the finish line. When emotion dissipates, we can call on discipline to help us reach our goals.

People often groan when they hear the word *discipline*, but it is not our enemy; it is our friend. The ability to discipline and control ourselves is a gift that God has given us. It is specifically for those times in life when emotion has vanished but we need to keep going.

Today's Thought

Discipline is your friend, not your enemy!

Dig Deeper into God's Word: Study 1 Corinthians 9:27; Hebrews 12:11

Starting Your Day Off Right

I rise before dawn and cry [in prayer] for help; I wait for Your word. (Psalm 119:147)

How do you start your day? Do you hurriedly get out of bed and barely make it out the door on time? Do you turn on the TV? Do you exercise? Whatever your morning routine may be, the most important question you can ask yourself is, *What role does God play when I start my day?*

I encourage you to spend time each morning focusing on God and His goodness in your life. Think about the dangers and difficulties He has brought you through, the ways He's healed and changed you, and how good it is to know that He cares for you and hears your prayers.

When you learn to set your mind on God each morning, He'll give you all the grace, peace, and joy you need for whatever you need to deal with throughout that day.

Today's Thought

If you make God your number one pursuit, He will add all the other things you need for the day.

Dig Deeper into God's Word: Study Psalm 145:2;
    Psalm 5:3

You Have a Friend in Jesus

But there is a [true, loving] friend who [is reliable and] sticks closer than a brother. (Proverbs 18:24)

The Bible offers great hope to any person who has been rejected and left feeling unwanted. Jesus understands that pain because He experienced it Himself.

Jesus understands the feelings that come when people push you away and make you feel devalued. He was rejected by men, too. Perhaps that is why Jesus used the final verse in the book of Matthew to tell His disciples, "And lo, I am with you always [remaining with you perpetually—regardless of circumstance, and on every occasion], even to the end of the age" (Matthew 28:20).

In His final moments on earth, Jesus wanted us to know that we are never alone. Though others might reject or abandon us, He never would. Jesus is with us in every situation, on every day, no matter what.

Today's Thought

You need not fear the rejection of man, because you have a friend in Jesus.

Dig Deeper into God's Word: Study John 15:13; Hebrews 4:15

Waking Up with Enthusiasm

For we have heard of your faith in Christ Jesus [how you lean on Him with absolute confidence in His power, wisdom, and goodness], and of the [unselfish] love which you have for all the saints (God's people). (Colossians 1:4)

Faith is leaning entirely on God in absolute trust and confidence in His power, wisdom, and goodness. Faith believes what it cannot yet see. It believes in its heart, not with its eyes.

You can choose to believe in your heart that something wonderful is about to happen to you and those you love. Believe that God's power is in you and that you need not fear anything because He has promised to be with you always.

Wake up each morning with an enthusiasm for the day. You might not awake every day feeling especially enthusiastic, but if you decide to believe and expect good things, enthusiasm will begin to fill your soul.

Today's Thought

The belief that all things are possible with God fuels enthusiasm for life.

Dig Deeper into God's Word: Study Ephesians 5:14;
    Romans 13:11

Living in Peace

Peace I leave with you; My [perfect] peace I give to you; not as the world gives do I give to you. Do not let your heart be troubled, nor let it be afraid. [Let My perfect peace calm you in every circumstance and give you courage and strength for every challenge.] (John 14:27)

We must refuse to live our lives trying to figure everything out all of the time. I've learned this firsthand. In the early years of my ministry, I was constantly frustrated because I was trying to figure everything out. I thought I just *had* to know how things were going to work out. I worried, reasoned, and wondered all day every day, and it was useless.

My husband, Dave, found it easy to trust God. He would simply cast his care and say that God would take care of it. Dave enjoyed his life while he patiently waited on God. What a great example he was for me!

We can choose to live in peace. We don't have to allow ourselves to be agitated and disturbed. Isn't that good news? Whatever you're waiting for today, use your quiet time with God to choose peace. God is going to bring His perfect plan to pass in your life. Relax and enjoy the journey.

Today's Thought

Don't forfeit your peace worrying about things you can't change and trying to make things happen that only God can make happen.

Dig Deeper into God's Word: Study Luke 12:22–23; Philippians 4:6–7

Are You Willing to Change?

Moreover, I will give you a new heart and put a new spirit within you, and I will remove the heart of stone from your flesh and give you a heart of flesh. (Ezekiel 36:26)

One of the easiest things for people to do is find fault with each other, but it is also one of the saddest. We all have flaws, and yet it seems that in our pursuit to change other people, we become blind to the things in ourselves that need to change.

Only God can truly and effectively change anyone, because change is something that must be done from the inside out. Our hearts must change in order for our behavior to truly change, and only God can give us a new heart.

When we receive Jesus as our Savior, God puts His heart and Spirit in us. He takes the hard, stony heart out of us and makes us sensitive to His will and touch. If someone you know is frustrating you, ask God to enable you to see them the way that He does, and it will help you to be patient with them. Instead of criticizing others, let God change you, and be a good example to those around you who also need to change.

Today's Thought

Be as patient with other people as you want them to be with you.

Dig Deeper into God's Word: Study John 3:3;
    Matthew 18:3

In Order to Give,
You Must Receive

Freely you have received, freely give. (Matthew 10:8)

In our society today, we find very few people who are able to freely give. Perhaps the above scripture sheds light as to why. If we never learn to freely receive from Jesus, we will never learn to freely give to others.

The devil tries to deceive us into believing that we must earn or pay for everything. We have somehow been convinced that we must struggle and strive to get what we want from God. Yet, Jesus said, "Come to Me, all who are weary and heavily burdened [by religious rituals that provide no peace], and I will give you rest [refreshing your souls with salvation]" (Matthew 11:28).

"Come to Me" is a comforting invitation. It is not filled with sounds of struggle and effort. Receive mercy and you can be merciful and receive God's love, and then you can love others.

Today's Thought

Regularly sit in God's presence and receive His forgiveness, love, and mercy.

Dig Deeper into God's Word: Study Titus 3:5;
    Romans 3:23–24

Doing Your Best

So that you may learn to recognize and treasure what is
excellent [identifying the best, and distinguishing moral
differences], and that you may be pure and blameless until
the day of Christ [actually living lives that lead others
away from sin]. (Philippians 1:10)

God is excellent. As His representatives, we should strive to be
excellent, too. It's important that we do our best in everything we
put our hands to. Always do more than enough rather than merely
doing barely enough.

Three ways to practice excellence are to keep your word and
always do what you tell people you will do, finish what you start,
and always be honest and truthful.

Paul urges us to learn to prize what is excellent and of real value.
As we make excellence a way of life, we will have God's joy and be
good examples to the world.

Today's Thought

Excellence is not perfection—it is simply doing the best
you can.

Dig Deeper into God's Word: Study 2 Timothy 2:15; 2
    Corinthians 5:20

God Promises to Take Care of You

The fear of man brings a snare, but whoever trusts in and puts his confidence in the Lord will be exalted and safe. (Proverbs 29:25)

God is good, and He always has our best interests in mind. He promises to take care of us if we trust Him to do so. You will see God's promises fulfilled in your life when you step out in obedience to follow His plan for you.

In your quiet time with God, believe in your heart and confess with your mouth that you trust God to take care of you and that you will not fear what man can do to you. You may *feel* fear at times, but you don't have to let the feeling control your actions or decisions. Feel the fear and do what you know you should do anyway.

Don't let man be large in your eyes and God small. God is greater than all men put together millions of times over. He created all that we see in this universe with a word, and surely He can take care of you.

Today's Thought

God is for you, and if He is for you, then it makes no difference who or what is against you.

Dig Deeper into God's Word: Study Isaiah 41:13; 1 John 4:18

Sharing Your Faith

And He said to them, "Follow Me [as My disciples, accepting Me as your Master and Teacher and walking the same path of life that I walk], and I will make you fishers of men." (Matthew 4:19)

When you are looking to tell others about your relationship with God, learn to let Him put you in the right place at the right time and open the door for you to share your faith. Sometimes that door opens very quickly, and at other times it can take a long time before the right opportunity comes to talk to them.

While you're waiting for the right time for a conversation, the way you live your life can be an effective witness of God's love and grace. Eventually people become curious or have a need in their lives that provokes them to be open to talking to you. Once their hearts are open and have been prepared by God, the rest is easy.

Pray for God to give you opportunity, and when the door is open, go in boldly, sharing all the wonderful things God has done in your life.

Today's Thought

Let people see Jesus through you!

Dig Deeper into God's Word: Study Matthew 28:19;
        Acts 1:8

Your Attitude Determines Your Altitude

God, your God, has anointed You above Your companions with the oil of jubilation. (Psalm 45:7)

It's one thing to have a goal, but in order to see that goal become a reality, there are accompanying action steps you have to take. And one of those steps is having the right attitude.

I'm sure you've heard the expression *Your attitude determines your altitude*. Well, this expression is popular for a reason—it's absolutely 100 percent right! You'll never be a confident, successful, happy person with a doubtful, defeated, sour attitude.

The first step to take in order to realize any goal is to adjust your attitude. Instead of thinking, *I can't*, choose to think, *I can do all things through Christ!* (see Philippians 4:13).

Today's Thought

When you're tempted to think, This is too hard, *just remind yourself that your attitude determines your altitude.*

Dig Deeper into God's Word: Study Romans 15:5; Proverbs 15:13

You Don't Have to
Wait for "When"

This [day in which God has saved me] is the day which the Lord has made; let us rejoice and be glad in it. (Psalm 118:24)

So many people have the mindset that they will be really happy and enjoy life *when* they go on vacation, *when* the kids get older, *when* they get higher on the ladder of success at work, *when* they get married... The list goes on and on. But you can enjoy your life with God now.

- You may be having a tough day, but don't wait until tomorrow to find some joy. Look for something good in each day.
- You may not have any extra money to spend right now, but that doesn't mean you can't do something you enjoy.
- You may have a two-year-old who makes you feel like you want to run away and hide, but try to settle down and enjoy this stage in their life, because it will only happen once.

You can enjoy and even love your life. You don't have to wait for "when"; you can do it today.

Today's Thought

You will never get this day back, so be sure to enjoy it now.

Dig Deeper into God's Word: Study Hebrews 6:11–12; Proverbs 19:15

Strengthen and Encourage Yourself

David strengthened himself in the Lord his God. (1 Samuel 30:6 NKJV)

If you've dealt with discouragement in your life, you know it can steal your zeal and joy. It makes us believe that we will fail before we have even tried to succeed.

In the Word of God, we see that David dealt with discouragement, but he didn't let that feeling control his life. He stood up to discouragement, refusing to be captive to it. He *strengthened himself in the Lord.*

You can do the same thing. You don't have to live captive to the feelings of discouragement any longer. The next time you begin to feel despair or discouragement, tell yourself: *I refuse to live in discouragement. God is good, and He wants me to enjoy my life. I am going to hope in God and expect something good to happen at any moment!*

Today's Thought

Encourage someone else today and trust God to strengthen you.

Dig Deeper into God's Word: Study Isaiah 40:29;
   Psalm 62:2

Worship Is Powerful

*O come, let us worship and bow down, let us kneel before the
Lord our Maker [in reverent praise and prayer]. (Psalm 95:6)*

Worship is an important part of any quiet time with God. Sometimes, when we are going through something difficult, stress and
frustration try to keep us from worshipping God. It's easy to get so
preoccupied with our problems that we forget the promises of God.

But when we remember the goodness, mercy, and faithfulness
of God, it is easy to worship Him. As you spend time with God, be
sure that you fellowship with *Him*, not with your problems.

Remember, God is good even when our circumstances are not.
Worshipping God helps us win our battles. Satan is not afraid of
our worry, but he is afraid of our worship.

Today's Thought

*Throughout the day in the midst of all you have to do, pause
briefly and simply whisper, "Lord, I love You!"*

Dig Deeper into God's Word: Study Luke 4:8;
    Psalm 96:9

Let God Do the Heavy Lifting

*I am the Vine; you are the branches. The one who remains
in Me and I in him bears much fruit, for [otherwise] apart
from Me [that is, cut off from vital union with Me] you can
do nothing. (John 15:5)*

A friend of mine hurt his back recently, and he is using wisdom
now and asking for help when he has something heavy to lift. Too
often we try to fix things ourselves and fail to ask God to help us
do the heavy lifting. Jesus said in John 15:5, "Apart from Me...you
can do nothing."

We may try to be self-sufficient, but we need to let God supply the grace and ability to do what we need to do. Willpower and
determination can only get us so far; they won't last forever, and we
can avoid many failures by asking for help.

We aren't meant to function apart from God. With Him, we can
do anything we need to do. Be humble enough to ask for God's help
rather than trying to do it all on your own.

Today's Thought

*"Help me, Lord!" is one of the most powerful prayers you
can pray.*

Dig Deeper into God's Word: Study Psalm 50:15;
    Hebrews 13:6

Speaking Positive Words

Pleasant words are like a honeycomb, sweet and delightful to the soul and healing to the body. (Proverbs 16:24)

The words we use when we talk to and about others affect us as much as they affect them. We can actually encourage ourselves by encouraging others. Words are seeds that we sow, and what we sow always brings a harvest in due time.

Pleasant words can bring healing to a broken heart, and hope to those who are hopeless. Words are more powerful than we might realize, and today is a good day to make a commitment to speak positive, life-filled words.

If you change your words, you can change your life.

Today's Thought

Let God use your words today to make a difference in the lives of others.

Dig Deeper into God's Word: Study Psalm 34:13;
        Proverbs 18:21

The Uniqueness of You

I will praise You, for I am fearfully and wonderfully made; marvelous are Your works, and that my soul knows very well. (Psalm 139:14 NKJV)

Nothing good comes from comparing yourself to someone else—trying to imitate, compete with, or outdo others. The more you compare your life to that of those around you, the less you'll enjoy the life God has given you.

God didn't create you to be like someone else. He created you to be unique and special, so why would you try to be anything other than who you are?

You are handcrafted—fearfully and wonderfully made. God has specially and uniquely qualified you to do something no one else can do. Stay encouraged. God has something special planned for your future. Resist the temptation to compare yourself to other people. Trust God and allow Him to use you in ways that are unique to you.

Today's Thought

The things in your life that make you different aren't hindrances; they are assets.

Dig Deeper into God's Word: Study Jeremiah 1:5; Isaiah 64:8

Happiness Is a Choice

*Blessed (happy, fortunate) are all those who long for Him
[since He will never fail them]. (Isaiah 30:18)*

I have discovered that joy—and even happiness—is a choice. We
can make the decision in our daily quiet time with God to enjoy
our lives regardless of the environment around us.

You don't have to let problems or challenges have the final say.
When the situation looks bleak, when the frantic pace of life seems
exhausting, you can still say, "I choose to enjoy my day. It is a day
that God has given me and I refuse to waste it being unhappy."

It might not seem natural at first, but don't give up. Keep choosing joy and happiness until it becomes a second nature. Eventually,
the daily struggles and pressures of life won't preoccupy your mind
anymore. You'll finally be able to enjoy the life that Jesus came to
give you.

Today's Thought

*Peace and happiness don't happen by accident. These are
choices you get to make each day.*

Dig Deeper into God's Word: Study Psalm 84:12;
    Proverbs 3:13

Your Worth Is Found in Christ

He brought me up out of a horrible pit [of tumult and of destruction], out of the miry clay, and He set my feet upon a rock, steadying my footsteps and establishing my path. (Psalm 40:2)

When our security is found in Christ and we no longer feel that we have to perform in order to have value, we are set free from fear. As long as we have deep-rooted fears about ourselves and our worth and value, we will have fear in many other areas of life.

Knowing who we are in Christ and accepting and loving ourselves because God accepts and loves us are the keys to living victoriously over those fears.

With Jesus, we can do all things—we are strong in Him, accepted in Him, made right with God through Him, justified in Him, and forgiven through Him. It feels good not to feel pressured to impress anyone, so remember that your worth is in Christ, not in what other people think of you.

Today's Thought

The unconditional love of God is the cure for those who are insecure.

Dig Deeper into God's Word: Study 1 Corinthians 6:11; John 3:16

Praying for Someone Else

First of all, then, I urge that petitions (specific requests), prayers, intercessions (prayers for others) and thanksgivings be offered on behalf of all people. (1 Timothy 2:1)

Just as our relationships are an important part of our social lives, they should be equally or more important in our prayer lives. When we pray *for* the people around us, these are prayers of intercession.

Many people do not know how to pray, nor do they have anyone in their lives who is praying for them. We can be a secret blessing to multitudes of people by simply praying for them. If they have a need, ask God to meet it; if they are sick, ask God to heal them; and if they need to make a decision, ask God to guide them.

I encourage you to use part of your quiet time with God to pray for other people. God can use you and your faith to change lives if you let the Holy Spirit guide you.

Today's Thought

Praying for someone is one of the greatest gifts you can give to them.

Dig Deeper into God's Word: Study Hebrews 13:18; James 5:13–18

Raise Your Expectations

Wait for and confidently expect the Lord; be strong and let your heart take courage; yes, wait for and confidently expect the Lord. (Psalm 27:14)

We say that a pregnant woman is expecting. That's why she starts making plans. She is acting on her expectation—buying clothes and bottles, setting up the crib, and preparing the nursery.

We can be people of faith who are expecting. We can get up in the morning making plans for God to do something great. With God's help, we can think, *Today may be the day. This is the day the Lord has made, and something great is going to happen to me.*

Even if God doesn't do exactly the thing you're asking for, try to broaden your view. Maybe you're asking for one thing, but God has something better in mind. Don't just ask for good; believe and have an expectation for *great*.

Today's Thought

God is good, and I am expecting Him to help me today with everything I have to do.

Dig Deeper into God's Word: Study Micah 7:7,
    Hosea 12:6

An Abundance of Goodness

How great is Your goodness... which You have prepared for those who take refuge in You. (Psalm 31:19)

We serve a good God, and He wants to flood your life with good things. If you go through each day worrying about how a bill is going to be paid, afraid you're not going to get the promotion at work, or bitter about what someone said behind your back, you're not living like a child who understands how good God really is.

Worry, fear, and bitterness are character traits of the old you. The new you can trust, be confident, and forgive, because you believe God can take anything that happens to you and work it out for your good—He has good things stored up for you.

Embrace the new you, realize you have a great inheritance in God, and get your hopes up about what God is going to teach you and how He is going to provide for you in any situation.

Today's Thought

Don't worry or fear you won't have enough; God is going to provide His very best for you.

Dig Deeper into God's Word: Study Psalm 145:9;
Psalm 34:8

Prisoner of Hope

Return to the stronghold, you prisoners of hope. Even today I declare that I will restore double to you. (Zechariah 9:12 NKJV)

I love the description "prisoners of hope." Think about it. If you're a prisoner of hope, you have no choice about it: You can't be negative, you can't be a worrier, and you can't be hopeless.

When times are tough, and when you're dealing with disappointment, the hope that surrounds you will cause you to rise up in faith.

Everything around you is telling you God can make a way, and when that happens, something stirs in your spirit. You are emboldened to believe and declare, "Good things are happening to me and through me."

I love the thought of being so hopeful that we can be surrounded by our hope in God. Are you ready to live your life full of hope and faith in God's promises?

Today's Thought

If you are steadfast in your hope, you can't lose, because God can't lose. Since God is for you, the victory is sure.

Dig Deeper into God's Word: Study Acts 2:26;
    Psalm 25:5

Sowing and Reaping

Whatever a man sows, this and this only is what he will reap. (Galatians 6:7)

The Word of God plainly tells us that we will reap what we sow. This principle applies to every area of our lives, including the way we treat others. Our attitudes and words are seeds we sow each day that determine what kind of fruit or harvest we'll have in our relationships.

The devil loves to keep us busy thinking selfishly, sowing words of strife in our families, and thinking negatively about others. He wants us to sow bad seed.

Let me ask you: What are you sowing today? With God's help, make the choice to sow love, forgiveness, kindness, and patience in every relationship and situation. You'll find that as you treat others the way God wants you to, you will reap a life filled with encouraging, godly relationships.

Today's Thought

In your quiet time with God, ask Him to show you practical ways you can sow good seeds in your relationships today.

Dig Deeper into God's Word: Study 2 Corinthians 9:6; Luke 6:38

Progressing in Prayer

But when you pray, go into your most private room, close the door and pray to your Father who is in secret, and your Father who sees [what is done] in secret will reward you. (Matthew 6:6)

Prayer is progressive and we all move from one level to another. No one ever masters prayer, because there is no limit to the depth of relationship we can have with God. It just keeps growing, keeps going deeper, and keeps getting stronger.

Our ability to pray develops and improves over time. We never become certified experts in prayer, and we never stop learning to communicate with God. Our experiences just keep getting richer and better.

You may not have arrived at your final destination, but you can thank God you are on the pathway that will take you there. As long as you are making progress, it really does not matter if you are crawling, walking, or running. Just keep pressing on!

Today's Thought

In every area of your relationship with God, He allows you to begin wherever you are and then helps you grow.

Dig Deeper into God's Word: Study Luke 11:2–4; Mark 11:25

Better than You Realize

Look at the birds of the air; they neither sow [seed] nor reap [the harvest] nor gather [the crops] into barns, and yet your heavenly Father keeps feeding them. Are you not worth much more than they? (Matthew 6:26)

Unless we intentionally focus on the blessings of God during our quiet time with Him, it can be easy to take those blessings for granted. I encourage you to fix your focus and begin seriously considering all the ways God is helping, protecting, and providing for you.

Are you breathing today? If so, you are a recipient of God's goodness. Do you have a home, a job, family, and friends? If the answer is yes, then you are experiencing the blessings of God. Do you have food to eat, clean water to drink, and clothes to wear? If so, you are blessed!

Perhaps you don't have *all* of these things, but you do have *some* of them, and you can rejoice in what you do have. I can assure you that no matter how difficult your circumstances are right now, there are many things in your life that are better than you may have realized.

Today's Thought

Count your blessings and thank God for every good gift in your life.

Dig Deeper into God's Word: Study James 1:17; 2 Corinthians 9:8

No More Excuses

Zaccheus stopped and said to the Lord, "See, Lord, I am [now] giving half of my possessions to the poor, and if I have cheated anyone out of anything, I will give back four times as much." (Luke 19:8)

In order to experience spiritual growth and maturity, we have to stop making excuses. Excuses for a poor attitude, excuses for a quick temper, excuses for a lack of initiative, excuses for that decision to quit—all of these (and more) will keep you from experiencing a joy-filled, overcoming life in Christ.

If you will face your problems, own up to your mistakes, make restitution where possible, and ask God to help you make the necessary changes in your life, you'll be amazed at how much more you'll enjoy every single day.

It's not easy to overcome fears, doubts, and dysfunction in order to move forward, but you don't have to let the previous *reasons* for your behavior become the present *excuses* for continuing that behavior. With God's help, you can choose to face your issues head-on and overcome your past rather than live in bondage to it.

Today's Thought

You can either live an excuse-filled life or a joy-filled life, but you can't live both.

Dig Deeper into God's Word: Study Exodus 4:10–12; Jeremiah 1:6–8

God's Power Takes Care of the Rest

My grace is sufficient for you, for My strength is made perfect in weakness. (2 Corinthians 12:9 NKJV)

When God puts a dream or a goal in your heart, there are steps you'll need to take to see it become a reality. If you have a dream, there is work to be done. You'll have to plan. There will be sacrifices you'll probably have to make. You'll need to persevere on days when everything in you wants to give up.

In other words, anytime you follow a dream God has given you, get ready to do everything in your power—everything you can do—to make it happen.

And here is the really good news: When your power seems insufficient, God's power takes care of the rest. If you do your part, God will always be faithful to do His part. Don't give up on your God-given dream when you feel too weak or incapable. God promises that His strength is made perfect in your weakness.

Today's Thought

You are never alone. God is with you, and He is faithful to give you the strength you need.

Dig Deeper into God's Word: Study Matthew 19:26; Psalm 28:7

Living in Truth

Rather, let our lives lovingly express truth [in all things, speaking truly, dealing truly, living truly]. (Ephesians 4:15 AMPC)

There is nothing more powerful than complete truth or "living truly." The truth of God's Word, the truth of who God says you are, the truth of healing and freedom, the truth of forgiveness and redemption—these are life-changing, revolutionary truths!

Just look at what the Word of God says about truth and how that truth can affect your life:

- "And you will know the truth [regarding salvation], and the truth will set you free [from the penalty of sin]" (John 8:32).
- "Jesus said to him, 'I am the [only] Way [to God] and the [real] Truth and the [real] Life; no one comes to the Father but through Me'" (John 14:6).
- "The Lord is near to all who call on Him, to all who call on Him in truth (without guile)" (Psalm 145:18).

In your quiet time with God, as you study His Word, build your life on the truths you find there. In Ephesians 4:15, Paul encourages us that we can live in the power of God's truth—we can be "living truly." What a great way to live!

Today's Thought

When you learn to find truth in your identity, your relationships, and your walk with God, everything changes for the better.

Dig Deeper into God's Word: Study John 16:13;
    Psalm 119:160

Prayer and Study

Be unceasing and persistent in prayer. (1 Thessalonians 5:17)

Your word is a lamp to my feet and a light to my path. (Psalm 119:105)

Prayer is one of the most important steps you can take. This is a way you can actively participate in faith each day. Thank God for what He is doing in your life, seek Him for His wisdom and guidance, and be honest with Him about your doubts and concerns. Prayer isn't a last resort—prayer is the first option.

Along with prayer, it is essential to spend time each day in the Word of God. Reading, studying, and meditating on Scripture fills you with faith and gives you the strength you need for the challenges of the day. This is a powerful action step that will propel you into what God is calling you to do.

Today's Thought

Spending time with God each day in prayer and studying His Word is the best thing you can do for yourself, your family, and all those you encounter every day.

Dig Deeper into God's Word: Study Luke 11:2–4; Hebrews 4:12

God Has a Wonderful Plan for Your Life

"For I know the plans and thoughts that I have for you,"
says the Lord, "plans for peace and well-being and not for
disaster, to give you a future and a hope." (Jeremiah 29:11)

The Word of God is very clear: God has a wonderful plan for your life. If you submit your heart to Him and give Him permission to have His way in your life, He is going to do something amazing.

You will never be left out, left behind, or forgotten. God's work always accomplishes more than you imagined, and this work always happens in His perfect timing.

When you face challenges or obstacles, decide in your heart that you won't get discouraged or defeated. Don't allow the daily problems you encounter to cause you to quit. Be a finisher in life! As long as you keep moving forward, you are going to see God's great plan for you come to pass.

Today's Thought

As a child of God, the only way you can be defeated is if you give up.

Dig Deeper into God's Word: Study Romans 8:28;
    Proverbs 3:5–6

The Spirit of a Conqueror

What then shall we say to all these things? If God is for us, who can be [successful] against us? (Romans 8:31)

No matter what you go through in life, if you have the spirit of a conqueror and you really know who you are in Christ and truly believe God is on your side, you do not have to be daunted or overwhelmed by any difficulty you may face.

Whether you are trying to pay off a mountain of debt, fight an illness, start your own business, or simply clean your house, you can do it with God on your side.

When confronted with a challenge, don't say, *I just can't do this anymore.* Instead, have the spirit of a conqueror and be bold enough to say, *God is for me. He is on my side, and I can do all things through Christ who strengthens me!*

Today's Thought

When you received Jesus as your Savior, you also received the spirit of a conqueror.

Dig Deeper into God's Word: Study Philippians 4:13; 2
   Corinthians 12:9

From the Old to the New

Therefore if anyone is in Christ [that is, grafted in, joined to Him by faith in Him as Savior], he is a new creature [reborn and renewed by the Holy Spirit]; the old things [the previous moral and spiritual condition] have passed away. Behold, new things have come [because spiritual awakening brings a new life]. (2 Corinthians 5:17)

Issues like insecurity, inferiority, regrets, and discouragement are things that you can confront and defeat as you move forward with God. With the help of the Holy Spirit, you can change these mindsets, but it will take some brave and bold choices on your part.

Old mindsets are part of the "old" that the apostle Paul says has "passed away." The good news is you no longer have to allow these hindrances of the past to affect your present or future.

Remember, God's plan for your life is not dependent on your circumstances, your doubts, or even your feelings—His plan is so much bigger than those things. Get an entirely new attitude and way of thinking today (see Ephesians 4:23). That is the road from the old life to the new.

Today's Thought

Every day with Christ is a new opportunity, a fresh slate, a brand-new beginning.

Dig Deeper into God's Word: Study Colossians
    1:13–14; Galatians 5:16

Keeping a Gratitude Journal

Bless and affectionately praise the Lord, O my soul, and do not forget any of His benefits. (Psalm 103:2)

Along with the Word of God, another thing you can meditate (focus, concentrate) on is a list of the good things God has done in your life. A great way to do this is to start a gratitude journal. This is just a journal you use to document the blessings of God that you are thankful for.

Many times we are frustrated and miserable over the course of the day because we think everything is going wrong. But the truth is that many things have gone *right*, and we just didn't realize them—or we forgot about them already.

If you make a conscious decision to look out for the good things each day so you can put them down in your gratitude journal, you'll have a much better day, and when you feel downcast, you can read your journal and recall the amazing things God has done in your life.

Today's Thought

You'll be surprised how much you have to be grateful for once you start to write your blessings down.

Dig Deeper into God's Word: Study Colossians 2:6-7; Psalm 138:1

Safe and Secure

No weapon that is formed against you will succeed; and every tongue that rises against you in judgment you will condemn. This [peace, righteousness, security, and triumph over opposition] is the heritage of the servants of the Lord. (Isaiah 54:17)

It is the will of God for His children to be secure and not to live in fear. We were created to feel safe, secure, confident, and bold; it's part of our spiritual DNA as born-again believers in Christ Jesus. But the key to living a secure life is knowing who you are in Christ, really receiving God's love for you, and basing your worth and value on who God says you are, not what you do.

According to Isaiah 54:17, part of our inheritance from God is security. We can be safe and secure in the knowledge that God's love for us is unconditional and unceasing.

Always remember that you are more than your job, your education level, or even your talents and abilities. You are God's very own; you belong to Him, and He loves you unconditionally. You can have a life of peace, joy, and true security because God is on your side.

Today's Thought

In your quiet time with God today, take a few moments to focus on the wonderful truth that God loves you—His love is perfect and is a free gift.

Dig Deeper into God's Word: Study Proverbs 18:10; Proverbs 30:5

Resisting the Temptation to Quit

*When He arrived at the place [called Gethsemane], He said
to them, "Pray continually that you may not fall into temptation." (Luke 22:40)*

The temptation to quit is part of being human, but giving in to it is
equal to giving up. We do not avoid temptation by sitting still and
refusing to deal with it or wishing God would remove it. As long as
we follow Jesus, our job is to resist temptation.

I encourage you to recognize the temptation to quit as a work
of the enemy, and to start resisting each temptation with everything in you. Don't let the devil lure you into passivity or wait until
you've been in a discouraged, hopeless slump for three days before
you act. Resist the devil at his outset. Declare war against temptation, and make the decision that you will never, ever quit doing
what God has called you to do.

Today's Thought

*If you take at least one step each day in the direction God
has called you, you will never be a quitter.*

Dig Deeper into God's Word: Study Romans 5:3–4; 1
    Corinthians 16:13

A Prayer of Petition

Delight yourself in the Lord, and He will give you the desires and petitions of your heart. (Psalm 37:4)

Petition is usually based on a desire. I believe that we have to desire something before we ask God for it. God puts the right desires in our hearts, and we have to know the difference between the desires of our flesh and the true desires of our hearts.

Sometimes a prayer is not answered because our prayers are related to a fleshly desire and are not really being led or inspired by the Holy Spirit (see James 4:3).

When God puts a desire within us, we are responding properly when we pray, "God, I want that," and the Word of God says that God will give us the desires of our hearts if we delight ourselves in Him. In your quiet time with God, don't be hesitant to petition God for the hopes, dreams, and goals He has placed in your heart. He loves to answer those prayers.

Today's Thought

Ask the Holy Spirit to guide you as you bring your needs and desires before God.

Dig Deeper into God's Word: Study Luke 11:9;
    Matthew 21:22

Being Used by God

*But God has selected [for His purpose] the foolish things
of the world to shame the wise [revealing their ignorance],
and God has selected [for His purpose] the weak things of
the world to shame the things which are strong [revealing
their frailty]. (1 Corinthians 1:27)*

Who does God use? We often think it is only those with great skill
or popularity, but the Bible says that God picks the unlikely. He
uses common, ordinary people like you and me.

In your quiet time with God, ask Him how He wants to use
you to accomplish His purposes on the earth. If you are willing
to make yourself available, God can and will do something great
through you.

Every common person can be used mightily by God. You just
have to believe He can use you and be daring enough to embrace
the goals or vision He puts in your heart. You have been chosen by
God to do great things. Embrace your calling today.

Today's Thought

God isn't looking for ability; He is looking for availability.

Dig Deeper into God's Word: Study 2 Timothy 2:1–3;
Isaiah 6:8

Striving for Fullness

You will show me the path of life; in Your presence is fullness of joy; in Your right hand there are pleasures forevermore. (Psalm 16:11)

It is good to be content. It is a godly quality, but we don't want to be so satisfied that we never want to see change. The best plan is to be happy where you are, while you're on your way to where you are going.

Even in our relationship with God, we should always be hungry to know His Word more deeply and to know Him more intimately.

Don't be satisfied with a mediocre relationship with God. Make the effort to make it the best it can be. To be mediocre in any area of life is to be halfway between success and failure, and it is not the place God has ordained for His people. God wants you to have fullness of joy! Examine your life and your heart to honestly determine whether you are striving to have your very best life in Christ.

Today's Thought

There is a gold mine hidden in every life, but we have to dig to get to it.

Dig Deeper into God's Word: Study Lamentations 3:25; Proverbs 8:17

Hope Stirs You to Action

May the God of hope fill you with all joy and peace in believing [through the experience of your faith] that by the power of the Holy Spirit you will abound in hope and overflow with confidence in His promises. (Romans 15:13)

Hope is exciting because you have a part to play. You don't have to sit back, just waiting for an answer to fall from the sky. You can take your hopes to God; ask Him for wisdom, guidance, and direction; and then take real and practical steps toward your goal.

It doesn't matter how difficult the task may seem or what odds are stacked against you; let hope stir you to action, one day at a time.

You can always maintain a positive attitude and speak faith-filled words. You can recall other victories you have had in your life in the past and be encouraged by them. Victory will require determination and discipline, but the results will be dynamic.

Today's Thought

God helped David defeat a giant; He can do the same for you.

Dig Deeper into God's Word: Study Psalm 119:166; 2 Corinthians 1:10

Prayer: Your Number One Weapon

And Nehemiah prayed. (Nehemiah 4:4)

In the book of Nehemiah, we see that Nehemiah went through many difficulties as he worked to accomplish the task God had set before him. And in the Amplified Bible translation of Nehemiah 4:4, we find three words that are vitally important to remember when we are trying to stand through a storm: "And Nehemiah prayed."

When faced with all the attacks that came against him—the laughing, the anger, the rage, the judgment, the criticism—Nehemiah simply went to God in prayer.

This is a great example for us to follow. Pray every time you feel afraid or intimidated. Pray when you are offended, or when someone hurts your feelings. Pray after you are unfairly judged or criticized. If you do, this will keep you from feeling bitter or angry and will help you accomplish God's plan for your life.

Today's Thought

When dealing with opposition, spend your time praying for people rather than fighting them. Let God fight your battles for you.

Dig Deeper into God's Word: Study Mark 1:35;
        Acts 7:59

Being Decisive

Do not, therefore, fling away your [fearless] confidence, for it has a glorious and great reward. (Hebrews 10:35)

Indecision is a miserable state to be in and certainly is not a fruit of a life lived confidently in Christ. The apostle James said the double-minded man is unstable in all his ways (see James 1:8).

Being indecisive because you're afraid you'll make the wrong decisions will get you nowhere. How much time do you think we waste when we can't make up our minds?

With God's help, start making decisions without second-guessing yourself or worrying about the choices you make. In your quiet time with God, ask Him for wisdom and confidence so you can move forward boldly. Don't be double-minded or wishy-washy, because doubting your decisions after you make them will steal the enjoyment from everything you do.

Today's Thought

Make the best decisions you can and trust God with the results.

Dig Deeper into God's Word: Study Job 22:28;
   Zechariah 7:9

Simply Believe

Jesus said to him, "Because you have seen Me, do you now believe? Blessed [happy, spiritually secure, and favored by God] are they who did not see [Me] and yet believed [in Me]." (John 20:29)

Our relationship with God is not about our performance. It doesn't matter how perfect you try to be; your performance is not what God desires. Some people in a crowd asked Jesus what they needed to do to please God, and the answer Jesus gave was, "Believe in the One whom He has sent" (see John 6:28–29).

This is so simple that we often miss it. We think we have to perform in order to please God, but the truth is that God simply asks us to believe in faith.

More than anything, God wants us to trust Him and to believe His Word, believe His promises, and believe His goodness and His unconditional love for us. Jesus came to earth because of the great love of the Father—this is the foundation of our faith.

Today's Thought

You can get off the treadmill of trying to be perfect, because you cannot buy or earn God's love or His favor, not even with a perfect performance.

Dig Deeper into God's Word: Study Mark 5:36;
    Mark 11:23

The Will of the Father

Then Jesus explained: "My nourishment comes from doing the will of God, who sent me, and from finishing his work." (*John 4:34* NLT)

Jesus said that He found satisfaction in doing the will of His Father and finishing His work. I wonder how many people in the world are dissatisfied simply because they gave up on their dreams.

We should not be people who give up or are easily defeated. I really believe that if we stay close to God, we can press through things that oppose us.

God gives us the grace (power of the Holy Spirit) to do whatever we need to do in life. Don't merely try to push through difficulties in the strength of your own flesh, but learn how to be thoroughly dependent on God. He gives grace to those who are humble enough to receive it, but if we want to try it on our own, He will wait for us to exhaust our own efforts.

Today's Thought

True satisfaction in life is found in pursuing and accomplishing the will of God by His grace.

Dig Deeper into God's Word: Study Matthew 25:21; 2 Timothy 4:7

The Heart of a Finisher

Let us not grow weary or become discouraged in doing good, for at the proper time we will reap, if we do not give in. (Galatians 6:9)

It is important for everyone to have the heart of a finisher, but I believe it is especially important for God's children. After all, we represent Him, and He always finishes what He starts.

Is there anything in your life that you are tempted to give up on? If there is, I am asking you to reconsider. In your quiet time with God, pray and ask if He wants you to give up, and unless you are sure that He does, I recommend that you press on.

The only reason we should ever give up is if we realize somewhere along the way that we are not doing what God wants us to do. Don't let the fear of circumstances or the weariness of passing time cause you to give up. You might be tired of waiting, but pressing forward is much better than going back.

Today's Thought

The heart of a finisher trusts God and keeps moving forward regardless of how challenging circumstances become.

Dig Deeper into God's Word: Study 1 Corinthians 9:24; James 1:12

Rest for Your Soul

*Come to Me, all who are weary and heavily burdened [by
religious rituals that provide no peace], and I will give you
rest [refreshing your souls with salvation]. (Matthew 11:28)*

We have a deep need and desire to enter what Scripture calls *the
rest of God*. This is more than just a physical rest—it is also a spiritual, mental, and emotional rest.

Jesus said that if we come to Him, He will give us rest for our
souls. And the apostle Paul teaches us that we can enter the rest of
God if we trust and confidently rely on God (see Hebrews 4:3).

If we will receive it, God will give us peace and rest from any
fears and frustrations, thoughts of doubt and insecurity, and even
the daily grind of life. All we have to do is cast our cares on God
and trust Him. The moment we do, then and only then can we rest
from the weariness of our own works.

Today's Thought

*God loves you and is pleased with you because you are His
child. Rest in that truth today.*

Dig Deeper into God's Word: Study Genesis 2:2;
    Psalm 4:8

A Sense of Adventure

This [day in which God has saved me] is the day which the
Lord has made; let us rejoice and be glad in it. (Psalm 118:24)

Having a sense of adventure is crucial to enjoying the life God has
given you. Adventure doesn't have to be something expensive or
over the top—it can be simple and fun. Here are some examples:

- You can turn a trip to the park with your kids or grandkids
  into a treasure hunt. *Adventure!*
- You can shake things up on date night. Rather than going to
  the same restaurant and movie theater, explore a new place to
  eat and choose a new post-dinner activity. *Adventure!*
- Your job doesn't have to be boring. You can think outside the
  box and propose a new strategy or take initiative with a bold
  idea. *Adventure!*
- Rather than staying safe in your spiritual comfort zone, why
  not sign up to serve in a new ministry or set out on a mission
  trip? *Adventure!*

If you want to enjoy the life God has given you, one of the best
steps is to make every day some sort of adventure with Him.

Today's Thought

If you view each day of your life as a big opportunity rather
than a boring obligation, adventure comes alive!

Dig Deeper into God's Word: Study John 10:10;
    Psalm 9:2

Trusting God in Tough Times

When I am afraid, I will put my trust and faith in You.
(Psalm 56:3)

Putting your trust in God will be easier on days when life is going well, but on the days when things aren't going so well, it will be more challenging. If you are facing something really tragic or painful, it will also be difficult, but we should remember that God never tells us to do something without giving us the ability to do it as we trust in Him.

We can trust God day by day. Even if you have days when you must say one thousand times, "I will put my trust in God," it is worth doing. Not only does it honor God, but it lifts burdens off of us that we were neither equipped nor meant to carry. When we decide to trust God, we're making a total commitment to trust Him no matter how hard it is to do. We give Him the honor of trusting that He is in control and He knows what is best for our lives.

Today's Thought

Trust is tested when things become difficult or challenging.
In these times, put your total trust in God, knowing that He
has your best interest at heart.

Dig Deeper into God's Word: Study Psalm 46:1;
    Psalm 62:8

Patience Is Power

Constantly rejoicing in hope [because of our confidence in Christ], steadfast and patient in distress, devoted to prayer [continually seeking wisdom, guidance, and strength].
(Romans 12:12)

Patience gives us the power to enjoy life while we wait for the things we desire. Much of life is wasted being miserable about things we cannot change. If we can change something unpleasant, then we should do that, but if we cannot, then we should give it to God and be determined not to be miserable while we wait to see what He will do.

Each day we waste by being impatient is one we will never get back, and a wise and prudent person does not waste any of the time God has allotted him to be on this earth. Whatever God is going to do about your problems is not going to be hurried by your impatience. No matter how long you have to wait for God to act on your behalf, patience has the power to keep you joyful while you wait.

Today's Thought

Something is always happening even when we think that nothing is taking place.

Dig Deeper into God's Word: Study James 5:7–8; Colossians 1:11–12

With Confidence and
without Fear

Therefore let us [with privilege] approach the throne of grace [that is, the throne of God's gracious favor] with confidence and without fear, so that we may receive mercy [for our failures] and find [His amazing] grace to help in time of need [an appropriate blessing, coming just at the right moment]. (Hebrews 4:16)

The wrong view of God will keep you stuck. Whether you're stuck in pain, dysfunction, loneliness, uncertainty, or fear, the devil will lie to you about God in order to keep you in that place forever.

One of the biggest lies the devil tells us is that God is mad at us. He knows that if we fall for this lie that God is angry and disappointed in us, he can keep us from having a real relationship with God.

The Word of God tells us that God loves us unconditionally. It also says that we can come before God "with confidence and without fear." You won't find a harsh, cruel, angry God; you'll find His mercy and grace. He is a good Father who loves you and has good thoughts about you, and He is waiting to help you in your time of need.

Today's Thought

The Bible tells us that God is slow to anger and abounding in love (see Psalm 103:8). His love for you is abundant and never-ending!

Dig Deeper into God's Word: Study Proverbs 14:26;
    Proverbs 3:26

Living to Please God

*So that you will walk in a manner worthy of the Lord
[displaying admirable character, moral courage, and personal integrity], to [fully] please Him in all things. (Colossians 1:10)*

It's important to find time to help others and serve those around
you, but you can't live your entire life trying to impress or please
others. I've discovered that no matter how hard you try, for some
people, it will never be enough. There are some people who are
going to expect you to do more and more until you reach a breaking point.

One of the best things you can do is let go of your need to please
people. In your quiet time with God, ask Him to show you if your
willingness to help others is based on the right motivation. Are you
happy to serve, or are you actually trying to earn their approval?

Instead of living to please others, live your life to please God—
this is when you will find peace and rest for your soul. Let go of
the unrealistic expectations of man and choose to live each day for
God. His approval is the only approval you will ever need.

Today's Thought

*True contentment is found in a life lived for God, not a life
lived trying to impress, please, or measure up to the expectations of others.*

Dig Deeper into God's Word: Study 1 Thessalonians
2:4; Galatians 1:10

Don't Be Afraid to Step Out

He said, "Come!" So Peter got out of the boat, and walked on the water and came toward Jesus. (Matthew 14:29)

One of the things that keeps us from stepping out in faith is the fear that we will mess up. But the truth is that no one learns how to hear from God without making mistakes from time to time.

Don't be overly concerned about errors or imperfection. It's important that you don't obsess and live in worry over the decisions you must make. You are a fallible, imperfect human being, but you can rejoice and be confident because you serve an infallible, perfect God.

Learn from your mistakes, correct the ones you can, and trust God for His guidance and protection. If you feel that God is prompting you to give something away, help someone out, or make a change in your life, do it! Take some action and sow the seed. If you believe it is right, then do your best and trust God to do the rest.

Today's Thought

God has not given you a spirit of fear. When you feel Him prompting you in a certain area, ask Him for His help and then move with boldness.

Dig Deeper into God's Word: Study Luke 9:62;
     James 1:5

Only God Can Carry You Through

My flesh and my heart may fail, but God is the rock and strength of my heart and my portion forever. (Psalm 73:26)

When things get tough in life, there is a tendency in many of us to say, "I'll just take care of this myself." Sometimes it's because no one was around to help you when you were younger, so you've always had to be independent. Other times it's because you are a strong person, and it's easier to rely on your own strength.

But you weren't meant to go through life alone, and there are going to be times when your strength isn't going to be enough.

You're going to face situations where only God is strong enough to carry you through. Get in the habit of looking to Him now. Don't wait for an obstacle so big or a pain so deep to drive you to Him in desperation. Start saying in your quiet time each day, "Lord, today I look to You. I don't depend on my own strength or ability; I depend on You."

Today's Thought

The most important thing you can do is allow yourself to be totally and completely dependent on God.

Dig Deeper into God's Word: Study Psalm 94:17–19;
   Isaiah 65:24

Cast Your Care

Casting all your cares [all your anxieties, all your worries, and all your concerns, once and for all] on Him, for He cares about you [with deepest affection, and watches over you very carefully]. (1 Peter 5:7)

The Bible instructs us to "cast" our care. That word means to pitch or throw. Isn't that a great picture? We don't just take off our cares and set them in a chair beside us where we can pick them up again later; we cast them completely away. We throw them as far as we can, never to be picked up again. We cast them on God, and He takes care of us.

Don't focus on hopeless thoughts or worried mindsets. Cast each care on God the moment you sense its presence, and things in your life will begin to change. The worry and anxiety that used to weigh you down will suddenly have no power over you anymore. Now you can experience what Jesus calls "rest (renewal, blessed quiet)" for your soul (see Matthew 11:29).

Today's Thought

According to 1 Peter 5:7, the key to casting your care is to understand how much God cares about you.

Dig Deeper into God's Word: Study Matthew 6:27;
    Philippians 4:6–7

Clearing the Hurdle of Selfishness

*For where jealousy and selfish ambition exist, there is dis-
order [unrest, rebellion] and every evil thing and morally
degrading practice. (James 3:16)*

An obstacle in our walk with God is the fact that we can be selfish,
especially with our personal space and freedom. If we are going to
be committed to growing closer to God, we're going to have to sacrifice our selfish wants at times.

We often think freedom is being able to do whatever we want,
whenever we want to do it. But true freedom is living in obedience
to God and following His plan for our lives.

Not only does God want you to succeed, He created you to succeed. He has your best interests at heart. Don't allow selfishness to
cause you to miss out on God's best plan for your life. Set aside your
own personal desires, and ask God what He wants you to do and
how He wants you to do it.

Today's Thought

*Persistence requires us to discipline our feelings and do
what is right, no matter how we feel about it.*

Dig Deeper into God's Word: Study Philippians 2:3;
    1 Corinthians 10:33

Let Me Introduce You

For we are His workmanship [His own master work, a work of art], created in Christ Jesus [reborn from above— spiritually transformed, renewed, ready to be used] for good works. (Ephesians 2:10)

You are a wonderful person, and if you have suffered under the weight of shame in your life, allow me to reintroduce you to yourself. You need to meet the real you, because you have been deceived into thinking you are someone you are not.

You are a child of God. He loves you, His power is in you, and He will enable you to do whatever you need to do in life. You are a new creation and the righteousness of God in Christ. You have an assignment from God and a great future. Your past has been washed away by the blood of Jesus. You are equipped and empowered by God.

The Word of God says many wonderful things about you, and you can learn what they are by reading and studying it each day in your quiet time with God.

Today's Thought

Don't ever allow what someone else thinks or says about you to be the factor that determines your value, because what God says about you is the only thing that really matters.

Dig Deeper into God's Word: Study Ephesians 1:5;
    1 Corinthians 12:27

God Will Make a Way

Even the darkness is not dark to You and conceals nothing from You, but the night shines as bright as the day; darkness and light are alike to You. (Psalm 139:12)

Fear takes root in our lives when we allow ourselves to be convinced that there is no solution to our problem. How often do we say or hear others say, "There is just no way this is going to work out"? Just because we don't know the way doesn't mean that there is no way.

Jesus said of Himself, "I am the Way" (John 14:6 AMPC). And God said, "I will lead the blind by ways they have not known" (Isaiah 42:16 NIV).

God is capable of leading us in the dark, because dark is the same as light to Him. We may be in the dark about what is going on, but God is light, so He never dwells in darkness. No matter what you are facing today, choose to trust that God will make a way.

Today's Thought

Think of a time in your life when God has made a way for you when there seemed to be no way, and choose to believe that He will do it again.

Dig Deeper into God's Word: Study Isaiah 30:21;
     1 John 1:5

Right Thoughts in God's Waiting Room

Now the mind of the flesh is death [both now and forever—because it pursues sin]; but the mind of the Spirit is life and peace [the spiritual well-being that comes from walking with God—both now and forever]. (Romans 8:6)

Waiting on God can be difficult at times, especially if we have the wrong attitude and mindset. Instead of being negative and impatient, we can actively put our hope and faith to work, knowing that God is in control. Our thoughts and attitudes can keep us joyful while we are in God's waiting room.

Here are some examples of right thoughts:

- *I'm so excited to see what God is going to do.*
- *I believe God is working, even though I don't see a change yet.*
- *God loves me, and I know He will take care of my problem.*
- *Psalm 139 says that God is thinking about me all the time, so I know He has not forgotten me.*
- *I will not live in fear, and I will never give up.*

These are thoughts that can produce joy, even as we practice patience. If we think with the mind of the Spirit while we are waiting on God, rest and peace will be the natural by-product.

Today's Thought

We can think with the mind of the flesh or the mind of the Spirit, the choice is ours.

Dig Deeper into God's Word: Study Romans 8:25; Colossians 3:12

Expecting God's Best

For God alone my soul waits in silence and quietly submits to Him, for my hope is from Him. (Psalm 62:5)

Living with expectancy is important in the Christian life. We can expect things to improve, expect good news, and expect a breakthrough because we know that God is at work on our behalf.

God can bring sudden moments to your life, moments that are so powerful and so miraculous, they change everything. One word from God, one touch from His Spirit, one promise from His Word, being in the right place at the right time, can set your life on a new course. Things can change in your life in a moment.

Living with a positive expectancy is what faith is all about. And God's Word says that without faith, it is impossible to please God (see Hebrews 11:6). It pleases God when we expect His divine help rather than expecting trouble. So, a good question to ask yourself is, *What am I expecting today?*

Today's Thought

Hopeful expectation will keep you in a spiritual posture of faith, believing and trusting God's plan for your life.

Dig Deeper into God's Word: Study Proverbs 15:15; John 7:38

Fruitful Is Better than Busy

Walk in a manner worthy of the Lord [displaying admirable character, moral courage, and personal integrity], to [fully] please Him in all things, bearing fruit in every good work and steadily growing in the knowledge of God [with deeper faith, clearer insight and fervent love for His precepts]. (Colossians 1:10)

Are you busy doing things that aren't bearing fruit? Is busyness stealing your peace? Sometimes we get stuck in the routine of doing things just because we've always done them, no matter how exhausting they may be or how unnecessary they have become.

God never called us to be busy. He called us to be fruitful. Too much pointless activity doesn't bear fruit and only stresses us out.

I encourage you to take an inventory of what you do throughout the day. You might be doing something God's not asking you to do, or something He was asking you to do but isn't anymore. In your quiet time, let the Holy Spirit show you how to get rid of needless busyness so that you can bear more fruit.

Today's Thought

Be strategic and intentional about the events and activities you plan for the week ahead. What are the things that will be the most productive and bear the most fruit?

Dig Deeper into God's Word: Study John 15:16; Jeremiah 17:7–8

Watching What You Say

Whatever you do [no matter what it is] in word or deed, do everything in the name of the Lord Jesus [and in dependence on Him], giving thanks to God the Father through Him. (Colossians 3:17)

Have you ever considered that you might be making your problems worse by talking about them excessively? It's easy to focus on the things that aren't going right. It seems like so many of our conversations revolve around what's going wrong rather than what's going right.

The kids are sick. The traffic is terrible. My feet hurt. I can't afford that. The more we talk about what's going wrong, the more power we give it in our lives.

When you're going through a trying time, the best thing you can do is stop talking about how big your problem is and start talking about how big God is. In your quiet time, meditate on God's Word and speak His promises over your situation. Power comes pouring in when you focus on speaking about what can happen with God on your side.

Today's Thought

You may not always feel positive, but you can always choose to speak positive words.

Dig Deeper into God's Word: Study Proverbs 18:21;
   Psalm 19:14

Walking Out Your New Beginning

His [tender] compassions never fail. They are new every morning; great and beyond measure is Your faithfulness.
(Lamentations 3:22–23)

The greatest new beginning any of us can have is becoming a new creature in Christ (see 2 Corinthians 5:17). And a personal, intimate relationship with Jesus is the key to a restored life, healing in your soul, and the second chance to become everything you were created to be.

Whether you're just starting your life with God or you gave your heart to Him long ago, it's important to understand that growing in Christ is a process that takes time. It's like this: When babies are learning how to walk, they fall down many times. But they always get up and try again.

That's what God is asking us to do. No matter how many times we fall down in life, if we continue to get back up, eventually we'll get to the place where we need to be.

Today's Thought

God loves new beginnings, and if you need a fresh start, He has one for you.

Dig Deeper into God's Word: Study 1 Peter 1:3;
        Isaiah 43:18–19

Faith Is a Shield

*Above all, lift up the [protective] shield of faith with which
you can extinguish all the flaming arrows of the evil one.
(Ephesians 6:16)*

In battles of old, soldiers protected themselves with shields, and in
Ephesians 6:16, the Bible speaks of "the shield of faith." If faith is
compared to a shield, it must be a way to protect ourselves when the
enemy attacks. Isn't it wonderful that God has given us a spiritual
defense system?

However, just like an actual shield, His shield is only effective
when it is raised up. When the enemy attacks us with unpleasant circumstances or thoughts that cause us to feel afraid, we can
immediately lift up the shield of faith.

The way we do this is by deciding that we will put our confidence in God instead of trying to figure out our own way to victory. It is helpful to say out loud, "I trust God in this situation. My
faith is in Him!" Say it firmly, with conviction. Jesus talked back to
Satan by saying, "It is written," and quoting Scripture (see Luke 4),
and we can do the same.

Today's Thought

*Your faith will only yield results when you decide to put it
into practice.*

Dig Deeper into God's Word: Study Psalm 32:7;
    1 John 5:4

The Past Is Over

For I will be merciful and gracious toward their wickedness,
and I will remember their sins no more. (Hebrews 8:12)

God will lead us into the best life we can possibly have, but first we need to let go of our past mistakes. Hebrews 8:12 tells us that God remembers our sins no more.

There's not a thing about you or me that God doesn't know. We are no surprise to Him. Yet when we turn to Him, He still opens His arms and invites us into a relationship with Him. He is not scared off by our past mistakes; He loves us in spite of them.

God chooses not only to forgive all of our sins but also to forget them. We need to stop remembering what God has forgotten. Let the past go, and boldly look ahead to your future in Him.

Today's Thought

Your history is not your destiny. God loves you and has a wonderful plan for your life.

Dig Deeper into God's Word: Study 2 Corinthians
    12:8–9; Philippians 3:13

Your Right Standing before God

Filled with the fruit of righteousness which comes through Jesus Christ, to the glory and praise of God [so that His glory may be both revealed and recognized]. (Philippians 1:11)

Because of the work of His Son, God views us as being righteous before Him through Jesus Christ. God accepts and approves of us because we are in Christ, and we can learn to do the same thing.

In our own effort, we are prone to make mistakes and fall into sin, but in Christ, we are renewed and restored people who have been re-created in Christ Jesus. Because of Jesus, our standing before God is right and pure.

We are born again that we may do the good works that He has prearranged and made ready for us, that we may live the good life Jesus died for us to have (see Ephesians 2:10). God wants us to see ourselves the way He does. He wants us to understand that in Christ, we are righteous in His sight.

Today's Thought

Jesus gave you right standing before the Father. When you are tempted to feel like you are not good enough or you don't measure up, just remember who you are in Christ.

Dig Deeper into God's Word: Study 2 Corinthians 5:21; 1 John 3:7

Dealing with Criticism

Let everyone be quick to hear [be a careful, thoughtful lis-
tener], slow to speak [a speaker of carefully chosen words
and], slow to anger [patient, reflective, forgiving]; for the
[resentful, deep-seated] anger of man does not produce the
righteousness of God. (James 1:19–20)

At some time in life we will all face criticism, but it is possible to learn how to cope with criticism and not let it affect your life.

The apostle Paul set a great example for us to follow. Paul said that he was not concerned about the judgment of others. He knew he was in God's hands and that in the end he would stand before God and give an account of himself and his life. He would not stand before any man to be judged (see 1 Corinthians 4:3–4).

Even if you don't do everything right, God sees your heart. If you're attempting to live for God and trying to do your best for Him, God is pleased (see Matthew 22:37–40). Don't get caught up worrying about the criticism of others; God loves you. His love and approval is all you need.

Today's Thought

The criticism and approval of man comes and goes. Build
your life on your relationship with God, not on the opinions
of others.

Dig Deeper into God's Word: Study James 4:11;
    Galatians 6:1

Is Your Desire the Best Desire?

Father, if You are willing, remove this cup [of divine wrath]
from Me; yet not My will, but [always] Yours be done.
(Luke 22:42)

The fear of not getting what we want is a root cause of the difficulty
we have in learning how to trust God. Most of us are convinced
that the only way we can be assured of getting what we want is if
we take care of ourselves. This fear prevents us from completely
trusting anyone.

God always knows what is best for us. His thoughts and plans
for us are better than our own. Once we believe that, we can trust
Him and learn to trust others.

Trusting God doesn't guarantee that we will always get what
we want. However, if we don't, it is only because God has something better in mind for us. As we learn to want what God wants for
us even more than what we ourselves want, we can have peace of
mind in every situation.

Today's Thought

Our peace of mind rests on whether or not we are willing
to trust that God's will is better than ours, even if we don't
understand it in the moment.

Dig Deeper into God's Word: Study James 4:3;
    1 John 5:14

Living to Give

Do not neglect to do good, to contribute [to the needy of the church as an expression of fellowship], for such sacrifices are always pleasing to God. (Hebrews 13:16)

It can be a healthy exercise to ask ourselves, *What am I doing to help someone else?* Can you think of the last person you helped?

Of course, we usually help our families during our daily activities, or we give gifts at Christmas, but I'm talking about something beyond that. I'm talking about living to give. A joyous and meaningful life is not found in what we get but in what we give.

How many people do we know who need help, and yet we have not even considered being the one to help them? When we start asking these difficult questions, we can find our answers disappointing. However, we can always get reappointed and begin doing the right thing.

I want to encourage you to purposely help people in need. Look for them and find some way to help.

Today's Thought

In your quiet time with God, ask Him to show you who you can help today and how you can bless their lives.

Dig Deeper into God's Word: Study Proverbs 11:25; 2 Corinthians 9:11

God's Timing

For as the heavens are higher than the earth, so are My ways higher than your ways and My thoughts higher than your thoughts. (Isaiah 55:9)

Sometimes we pray and God helps and delivers us right away, but at other times His help comes on a timetable we do not understand. We wonder, *If I am going through something that causes me to suffer, and God is going to deliver me, then why wait for months or even years before doing so?*

Sometimes God waits to answer because we are asking the wrong questions or we are not ready to receive what we are asking for. No matter what your question may be, the answer is always the same: God knows what is best, and His timing is always perfect. Don't worry when things don't happen on your timetable. He is in control, and He is going to answer your prayer in His perfect timing.

Today's Thought

God sees the big picture. He knows things you don't yet know. Trust Him to work in His timing and believe that He will use this time of waiting to develop something powerful in your life.

Dig Deeper into God's Word: Study Habakkuk 2:3;
    Acts 1:7

Jesus Came to Lift Burdens

To give them beauty for ashes, the oil of joy for mourning, the garment of praise for the spirit of heaviness. (Isaiah 61:3 NKJV)

When we let God take our messes, He has the ability to turn them into miracles and use our mistakes for our good if we will only trust Him.

Isaiah 61:3 says that He will give us beauty instead of ashes, but I find that many people want to hold on to their ashes, the cinders of the past, as reminders of their shortcomings and failures. Let go of your ashes and reach for something new.

Do you need a second chance? In your quiet time with God, ask Him for a second chance or a third, fourth, or fifth—whatever you need. God is full of mercy and long-suffering. His loving-kindness never fails or comes to an end. He has removed your transgressions from you; you don't have to hang on to them anymore.

Today's Thought

Jesus came to lift burdens, but you must be willing to let them go and believe He is greater than your mistakes. Give Him your ashes today.

Dig Deeper into God's Word: Study Psalm 68:19; Psalm 81:6

Let the Storms Pass

God is our refuge and strength [mighty and impenetrable],
a very present and well-proved help in trouble. (Psalm 46:1)

We all face storms in life—some are like the quick afternoon storms
that are common in summer, and some seem like hurricanes. But
one thing is true about all storms: They don't last forever.

Thoughts and feelings run wild in the midst of our personal
storms, but those are exactly the times we need to be careful about
making decisions. Decisions are best made in our quiet times with
God, not in the midst of a storm.

Instead of drowning in worry and fear, get in touch with God,
who sees past the storm and orchestrates the big picture. God
makes sure everything that needs to happen in our lives happens
at the right time, moves at the appropriate speed, and causes us to
arrive safely at the destinations He has planned for us.

Today's Thought

When dealing with a personal storm, tell yourself, Let emotions subside before you decide.

Dig Deeper into God's Word: Study 2 Corinthians
4:17–18; Romans 8:18

When Change Occurs

There is a season (a time appointed) for everything and a time for every delight and event or purpose under heaven. (Ecclesiastes 3:1)

When we have unexpected change in our lives, or even planned changes, it often leaves us with many questions. We, of course, want to know the entire blueprint for our lives right away, but if we knew everything that would take place in the future, life would be boring as we live it out day by day or more frightening than not knowing.

God is good, and if knowing what is going to happen before it happens is the best thing for us, then He will arrange things to work that way. If He doesn't do that, we can safely assume that waiting and being surprised is the best thing for us.

If you struggle with new situations, let me recommend that you *change your mind about change.* The new things God brings will always produce some of the most positive opportunities, relationships, and personal growth you will ever experience.

Today's Thought

God knows all about everything that is happening in your life right now, and He has already planned a good outcome.

Dig Deeper into God's Word: Study Deuteronomy 31:8; Malachi 3:6

Defeating Doubt

But he must ask [for wisdom] in faith, without doubting [God's willingness to help], for the one who doubts is like a billowing surge of the sea that is blown about and tossed by the wind. (James 1:6)

Many times in life, we are opposed by thoughts and emotions that are intended to weaken our relationship with God. Doubt is one such feeling.

Feelings of doubt or uncertainty don't mean that we don't have faith and are not relying on God. It simply means that the devil is bringing temptation to stop us from putting our confidence in the Lord. We can consider the source of doubt and realize it is a lie.

We should "watch and pray" as we are instructed in God's Word (see Matthew 26:40–41). When we are faced with doubt, see it for the deception that it is. Take that doubt to God and ask Him to give you the strength to defeat it. Don't feed those doubts; feed your faith instead. Remember what God says about your life and your future, and choose to stand on those promises.

Today's Thought

We can only defeat our enemy when we recognize his tactics. Doubt is closely connected with fear, and both of these things are tools of the enemy.

Dig Deeper into God's Word: Study Jude 1:22;
   Mark 9:24

Attacking Your Problem

David ran quickly toward the battle line. (1 Samuel 17:48)

In 1 Samuel 17, all of the soldiers of Israel were too afraid to fight the enemy, Goliath. Everyone, that is, except for one teenage boy: David. David knew that his Provider was greater than his problem. So he did the unthinkable—he ran to the battle.

We can do the same thing. When facing a challenge or an obstacle, instead of shrinking back in fear, we can go on the offensive, knowing that God is on our side.

Be full of confidence today. In your quiet time with God, ask for His wisdom and guidance on how to go on the offensive. Speak positive, faith-filled words over your situation. Have an optimistic outlook. Go into your day knowing that no weapon formed against you shall prosper (see Isaiah 54:17).

Today's Thought

Confront your problems instead of shrinking from them in fear and you will see that God is on your side and you are more than a conqueror.

Dig Deeper into God's Word: Study Psalm 18:29;
    Psalm 27:3

Whom Can You Encourage Today?

Therefore encourage and comfort one another and build up one another, just as you are doing. (1 Thessalonians 5:11)

People love to be blessed and encouraged. It can completely change someone's entire day. Heartfelt compliments help people feel and perform better, while faultfinding makes them perform worse.

Choose someone today whom you would like to bless, and begin to encourage them. Tell them how much you value them, how special they are to the Lord, and how thankful you are for them. I believe you will be amazed at the results.

What frequently happens is that the person being encouraged is so grateful for the encouragement, they reciprocate with kindness and appreciation. They are doing it because they see the example you are modeling and they return the favor. Better yet, they will turn around and look for other people to encourage, too.

Today's Thought

When you focus on loving, blessing, and encouraging others, God will always bless you in return.

Dig Deeper into God's Word: Study 2 Thessalonians 2:16–17; 2 Corinthians 1:3–4

Living for God

For they loved the approval of men more than the approval of God. But Jesus loudly declared, "The one who believes and trusts in Me does not believe [only] in Me but [also believes] in Him who sent Me. (John 12:43–44)

Many people don't fulfill their destiny because they fear what others think of them. In order to do what God is leading us to do, we will often be misunderstood or even rejected by people. Jesus came to do the will of His Father in Heaven and to help mankind, yet He was rejected.

Doing the right thing doesn't always guarantee acceptance from people. At some point in life, every person must decide whether they will be a people-pleaser or a God-pleaser.

Our goal should be to please God, no matter what the cost. It may cost us our reputation, we may need to walk away from something we don't want to give up, or we may need to do something we don't want to do, but the rewards are always worth the sacrifice in the end.

Today's Thought

Being excessively concerned about what others think is a total waste of time, because we cannot completely control what they think anyway.

Dig Deeper into God's Word: Study Ephesians 6:6; Colossians 3:23

Dividing Soul and Spirit

For the word of God is living and active and full of power [making it operative, energizing, and effective]. It is sharper than any two-edged sword, penetrating as far as the division of the soul and spirit [the completeness of a person]. (Hebrews 4:12)

The dividing of soul and spirit is important. Our soul tells us what we want, think, and feel, but the Holy Spirit reveals God's will to us. Anytime we are making a decision, especially an important one, acknowledging God is the wise thing to do. If we acknowledge Him, it shows that we care about His will.

Studying God's Word helps us to know His heart (His will) on a variety of subjects and helps us stay on the right path in life. There are many decisions that we make each day, and God has given us the wisdom to do so, but letting Him know that we want His will even more than we want our own is a part of developing an intimate relationship with Him.

You and God are partners together in your life, and learning to walk with Him through life will ensure that you can enjoy the best life possible.

Today's Thought

Acknowledge God in all your ways, and He will direct your path.

Dig Deeper into God's Word: Study 1 Thessalonians 5:19; 2 Timothy 3:16–17

Rich in Mercy

But God, being [so very] rich in mercy, because of His great
and wonderful love with which He loved us, even when we
were [spiritually] dead and separated from Him because
of our sins, He made us [spiritually] alive together with
Christ. (Ephesians 2:4–5)

In His love, God chose us. He made us holy, consecrated, and blame-less in His sight, and He allows us to live before Him without reproach (any sense of guilt or shame). God does all this because He is good and He wants to bless us.

Instead of getting what we deserve as sinners, we are given the opportunity to stand forever in the presence of God. We are given right standing with Him. This is God's will because it pleases Him; it is His kind intention (see Ephesians 1:4–5).

Grace takes the punishment that we deserve, and mercy gives us blessings that we don't deserve. Believe it, receive it, and be gracious to all the people in your life.

Today's Thought

When we fail, we should never draw away from God, but
we should run to Him, for He is our only hope of recovery
from the error of our ways.

Dig Deeper into God's Word: Study Psalm 23:6;
    Romans 9:16

Root of Rejection

Come to Him [the risen Lord] as to a living Stone which men rejected and threw away, but which is choice and precious in the sight of God. (1 Peter 2:4)

If we've dealt with rejection in the past, it is amazing how that pain can affect our present and even our future. We approach life and relationships with a fear of being rejected rather than by faith that we are and will be accepted.

When you feel hurt, people are not always trying to hurt you. They may be insensitive or less thoughtful than they could be, but people who have experienced the pain of rejection often feel they are being attacked, even though that is not true. It is best to always believe the best of everyone. If you do, it will spare you a lot of pain and misery.

The next time you feel hurt by someone, ask yourself this question: *Is that person really trying to hurt me, or am I just allowing myself to feel hurt due to old wounds from the past?*

Today's Thought

There is no person who is liked by everyone, so enjoy the many who love and admire you, and believe the best of all the rest.

Dig Deeper into God's Word: Study Mark 8:31;
   Luke 6:22

Unshakable Confidence

*Yet in all these things we are more than conquerors and
gain an overwhelming victory through Him who loved us
[so much that He died for us]. (Romans 8:37)*

With God on our side, we can always have a sense of triumph. Paul
assures us in Romans 8:37 that through Christ Jesus, we are more
than conquerors. Believing that truth gives us the strength and
confidence we need in life.

In this world our confidence can be shaken when trials or difficulties come our way, especially if they are lengthy. But we can
have so much confidence in God's love for us that no matter what
comes against us, we know deep inside that we are more than conquerors. We may go through difficulties, but with God we always
win in the end.

Whenever a trial of any kind comes against you, choose to tell
yourself, *This too shall pass.* Be confident that during the trial, God
will teach and mature you in ways that will help you in the future.

Today's Thought

*Believe you are a winner in life, and see yourself as strong
and powerful in and through Christ.*

Dig Deeper into God's Word: Study 2 Corinthians 3:5;
    1 John 3:20–21

Releasing Your Faith

For we walk by faith, not by sight [living our lives in a manner consistent with our confident belief in God's promises].
(2 Corinthians 5:7)

One of the ways to release your faith is to do whatever you believe God is asking you to do, without hesitation. Obedience is a key to our victory and shows that we have placed our faith in God.

If we are hearers of the Word and not doers, we are deceiving ourselves through reasoning that is contrary to the truth (see James 1:22). Obedient action is a requirement if we want to see God move in us and through us.

There is no doubt that fear will come, but if you keep moving forward in obedience, it has no way to control you. Even though fear may be talking to you, that doesn't mean you have to listen. Do what God asks you to do, even if you have to do it afraid.

Today's Thought

True faith doesn't have to have all the answers ahead of time—it simply trusts and responds in obedience to the voice of God.

Dig Deeper into God's Word: Study 2 John 1:6;
    Luke 11:28

A Cheerful Giver

Let each one give [thoughtfully and with purpose] just as he has decided in his heart, not grudgingly or under compulsion, for God loves a cheerful giver [and delights in the one whose heart is in his gift]. (2 Corinthians 9:7)

One of the great joys in life is being generous—giving whatever we can whenever we can. And that doesn't just mean money. We can give help, encouragement, time, and forgiveness.

As Christians, we can reject selfishness and give from the love we have so readily received. If you think about it, when we give our lives to God, everything we have is His anyway—it no longer belongs to us. We should generously give of our resources the way God leads us to.

In your quiet time with God, ask Him to help you give cheerfully. It pleases Him, and as you learn to give with a cheerful heart, you will become happier, more fulfilled, and a daily blessing to all of those around you.

Today's Thought

A cheerful giver doesn't see giving as an obligation but as an opportunity.

Dig Deeper into God's Word: Study Matthew 5:42; Mark 9:41

Living with Discernment

And this I pray, that your love may abound still more and more in knowledge and all discernment, that you may approve the things that are excellent, that you may be sincere and without offense till the day of Christ. (Philippians 1:9–10 NKJV)

The gift of discernment is an important thing to have, and it is available to all those who have a relationship with God.

Here's how it works: Before you do anything, you can quickly check with your spirit to see if the thing you are about to do feels right. If you have peace, then proceed confidently. But if you are uncomfortable or confused, remain still. Ask God to give you His wisdom on how to proceed instead of rushing into something that you don't have peace about.

The exciting thing about moments like these is that every time you choose to listen to and follow the Holy Spirit's promptings, your spirit grows stronger in God, and more and more of God's wisdom is released in your life to operate in the fruit of the Spirit. When you seek to operate with discernment, God will guide you into His very best for your life.

Today's Thought

Yield to the Holy Spirit and follow His promptings, and you will grow in the same discernment that Jesus walked in.

Dig Deeper into God's Word: Study 1 Kings 3:7–10; Psalm 119:125

Have a Can-Do Attitude

I can do all things [which He has called me to do] through
Him who strengthens and empowers me. (Philippians 4:13)

Maybe you've gone through life thinking *I can't*, because that's what others have told you. If no one has told you previously, hear God saying now: *You can!*

Those are powerful words for you to read and believe, because as I like to say, miracles come in *cans*.

- You *can* overcome.
- You *can* make it through.
- You *can* forgive.
- You *can* raise godly children.
- You *can* get out of debt.
- You *can* experience joy.
- You *can* meet your goal.
- You *can* keep moving forward.

When facing any challenge—no matter how big it may seem—God will give you all the strength you need. You can do it!

Today's Thought

Armed with God's power, you can identify and eliminate
every can't *in your life and replace it with I* can.

Dig Deeper into God's Word: Study Ephesians 6:10–11;
    Nahum 1:7

Say What You Say on Purpose

Even a [callous, arrogant] fool, when he keeps silent, is considered wise; when he closes his lips he is regarded as sensible (prudent, discreet) and a man of understanding. (Proverbs 17:28)

There is a time to talk and a time to keep silent. Sometimes the best thing we can do is say nothing. When we do say something, it is wise to think first and be purposeful in what we say.

If you make a decision that you are going to say as little as possible about your problems and disappointments in life, they won't dominate your thoughts and your mood. And if you talk as much as possible about your blessings and hopeful expectations, your frame of mind will match them. Your words affect your attitudes and actions.

Be sure each day is filled with words that fuel joy, not anger, depression, bitterness, or fear. Talk yourself into a better mood. Choose to speak something positive in every situation.

Today's Thought

We can be purposeful about what we say with the help of the Holy Spirit and by applying principles of discipline and self-control.

Dig Deeper into God's Word: Study Psalm 141:3;
   Proverbs 13:3

Seeking God above Everything Else

Trust in and rely confidently on the Lord with all your heart and do not rely on your own insight or understanding. In all your ways know and acknowledge and recognize Him, and He will make your paths straight and smooth [removing obstacles that block your way]. (Proverbs 3:5–6)

If we seek to know *things*, we may never know God as we should, but if we seek to know *Him*, we can be assured that He will show us everything we need to know at the exact right time.

Instead of trying to figure everything out, we can trust God to reveal His wisdom and understanding to us at the right times. We are encouraged in God's Word to lean not on our own understanding but in all of our ways to trust God with our mind and heart. Go ahead and try it; you will start to enjoy life more than ever before.

Use the time you previously spent worrying, frustrated, and trying to figure everything out seeking to know God better. That is the best way you can spend your time; it comes with great rewards.

Today's Thought

It is amazingly refreshing when we finally decide to trust God and to cease from having to understand everything that is taking place in our life.

Dig Deeper into God's Word: Study Matthew 6:33; Psalm 27:4

Do It Afraid

Do not fear [anything], for I am with you; do not be afraid,
for I am your God. I will strengthen you, be assured I will
help you. (Isaiah 41:10)

Fear is an enemy that torments the soul and seeks to steal our peace
and joy. Totally conquering fear is not something that we do in one
day, or even a thousand days. It is something we conquer one day at
a time with God's help.

Fear can show up quite unexpectedly in many ways. One of our
goals should be to recognize it so we can deal with it promptly. You
can't defeat an enemy you don't know is there.

Being free from fear doesn't mean that we will never experience
it or be confronted by it. It means that we are committed to not
allowing it to rule our lives, and when necessary, we will do what
we need to do, even if we have to do it afraid.

Today's Thought

Ask God to help you recognize fear at its onset and keep
moving forward in His strength.

Dig Deeper into God's Word: Study Isaiah 43:1;
     Psalm 34:4

Victories Build Faith

It was for this freedom that Christ set us free [completely liberating us]; therefore keep standing firm and do not be subject again to a yoke of slavery [which you once removed]. (Galatians 5:1)

Knowing something mentally and knowing it by experience are two entirely different things. We often say that heart knowledge is much deeper than head knowledge. Faith builds in our heart as we exercise it, not just when we think about it.

Each obstacle that you confront with God's help becomes a small victory for you, and it prepares you to face the next one.

Whenever you complete a challenge or overcome an enemy, you will enjoy your new freedom so much that you will soon be totally unwilling to live any other way. You will soon be determined that your days of hesitation and quitting are over. That doesn't mean you won't face difficulties, but it does mean that you will be more and more determined to trust God and win the battle.

Today's Thought

Remembering past victories will help you face new challenges confidently.

Dig Deeper into God's Word: Study Psalm 119:45; 1
    Corinthians 15:57

Strength for Today

So do not worry about tomorrow; for tomorrow will worry about itself. Each day has enough trouble of its own. (Matthew 6:34)

The best way to face challenges is to deal with them one day at a time. Looking too far down the road only tends to overwhelm us. Trusting God requires that we believe He gives us our "daily bread"—that is, we receive what we need as we need it and usually not before.

Sometimes challenges can seem impossible and overwhelming, but God is always with us. We just need to be courageous and receive the strength He gives us. Remember that God will give you the grace to do what you need to do *today*, so it's important to focus on living in the moment rather than worrying about tomorrow.

Whatever you need to do—getting out of debt, solving a marriage problem, organizing your home, completing a project—you can do it with God's help, one day at a time.

Today's Thought

You are ready for anything and equal to any task, because God will always give you the strength you need.

Dig Deeper into God's Word: Study Matthew 6:11; James 4:6

Laugh It Off

Then our mouth was filled with laughter and our tongue with joyful shouting; then they said among the nations, "The Lord has done great things for them." (Psalm 126:2)

Too many times in life, we let some insignificant, minor irritation ruin our day. Even if we allow it to ruin an hour, or as little as five minutes, those are minutes we aren't enjoying the life God has given us.

It has taken a while, but with God's help, I've learned not to take everything in life so seriously. It's important to make time each day to have some fun and take advantage of every opportunity to laugh.

Laughter is vital in battling the stresses and worries that try to find their way into our lives.

Whether it's something as silly as spilling coffee or something as serious as a major life decision, if you decide to lighten up a little and not take everything too seriously, you'll be surprised at how quickly your stress will decrease and your joy will increase.

Today's Thought

You have a choice to laugh frustration off or store frustration up. Choose wisely.

Dig Deeper into God's Word: Study Job 8:21;
    Proverbs 31:25

Running in God's Strength

Let us run with endurance and active persistence the race that is set before us. (Hebrews 12:1)

Many people allow fear to freeze them in their tracks. Rather than running with confidence, springing toward the opportunities and challenges of life, they're sitting still, frozen in hesitation. Worry, anxiety, and stress are like anchors holding these people down.

But this doesn't have to be you. You can defeat fear and enjoy an exciting and adventurous life with God. If God is leading you to do something, it doesn't matter how unsure you may feel; you can move forward in faith, knowing God is with you and working on your behalf.

Fear, worry, and anxiety create stress, and stress steals our energy, but resting in God's love for you will energize you to do all you need to do.

Today's Thought

Confidence that God is working in your life will keep you from panicking when faced with a difficult situation.

Dig Deeper into God's Word: Study Nehemiah 8:10;
    Psalm 22:19

Truth Will Set You Free

And you shall know the truth, and the truth shall make you free. (John 8:32 NKJV)

Truth is wonderful. Jesus said it will make us free. But as wonderful as truth is, we must be willing to face it. Truth often shocks us into a reality we may feel unprepared to see, but if God is revealing it, He knows the time is right.

As tough as it might be to face the truth, especially when it requires that we make changes in our lives, it is always better than avoiding it. You will be so glad to live in the freedom and rewards it brings.

We can never get to where we want to be unless we truly face where we are. We must not look to the world to teach us how to live sincere, godly lives, but rather to the Word of God and the Holy Spirit. These are the real sources of truth—truth that will change us, encourage us, instruct us, and set us free.

Today's Thought

Things we hide from have power over us, but when they are exposed to the truth, we have power over them.

Dig Deeper into God's Word: Study John 17:17;
Psalm 145:18

God's Word Never Changes

*Let the word of Christ dwell in you richly in all wisdom,
teaching and admonishing one another in psalms and
hymns and spiritual songs, singing with grace in your
hearts to the Lord. (Colossians 3:16 NKJV)*

The more we study the Word of God, the more we begin to trust
His promises instead of our circumstances. When we choose to put
our faith in God, His Word has the final say. God's Word is the
truth you can base your life on!

- If your child or grandchild is making bad decisions, know that
  God can get them back on track (see Proverbs 22:6).
- When finances seem low, trust that God will provide every-
  thing you need (see Philippians 4:19).
- If you are dealing with the pain of a loss, you can rest assured
  that God will comfort and encourage you through this season
  (see 2 Corinthians 1:3–5).
- When you feel lonely, be strengthened in your heart, knowing
  God will never leave you or forsake you (see Deuteronomy 31:6).

Circumstances may change from day to day, but God's Word
never changes.

Today's Thought

*As you take time to meditate on God's Word and apply it to
your situation, His promises will work in your life.*

Dig Deeper into God's Word: Study Romans 10:17;
   James 1:22

Celebrate Your Successes

He brought me up out of a horrible pit [of tumult and destruction], out of the miry clay, and He set my feet upon a rock, steadying my footsteps and establishing my path.
(Psalm 40:2 AMP)

One of the reasons many people don't strive to achieve great things in their lives is because they feel bad about themselves. Feeling ashamed of who you are or suffering from abnormal guilt can easily steal your motivation.

If you don't like yourself, the bad feelings you have inside will be a continual source of pain that keeps you from moving forward. It is vital that you learn to accept and respect the person God made you to be.

Our behavior may be far from perfect, but if we are willing to change, God will keep working with us, and every day we can improve. Don't despise yourself because of your imperfections; instead, learn to celebrate your successes, even small ones, in order to keep moving forward in life.

Today's Thought

There is never one moment in your life when God does not love you!

Dig Deeper into God's Word: Study Psalm 47:1;
    Proverbs 16:3

Forgive Quickly

Be kind and helpful to one another, tender-hearted [compassionate, understanding], forgiving one another [readily and freely], just as God in Christ also forgave you. (Ephesians 4:32)

Learning to forgive quickly and completely is one of the most important keys to maintaining joy in our lives. Because God has forgiven us, He expects us to forgive others for their injustices against us.

Just as we can receive forgiveness from God and confidently trust that He is not angry with us, we can forgive others and not be angry with them. Anger and unforgiveness will quickly dilute your joy. It is impossible to be bitter and better at the same time.

Learning to be forgiving and merciful toward the faults of others is a sign of growing spiritual maturity—it is being obedient to God's Word. When we obey God, especially when it is difficult to do so, He will always reward us with peace and joy.

Today's Thought

Holding on to bitterness or unforgiveness toward someone doesn't hurt them—it only hurts you. Allow God to be your vindicator.

Dig Deeper into God's Word: Study Matthew 6:14;
    Luke 6:37

Be an Answer to Someone's Prayer

Do not merely look out for your own personal interests, but also for the interests of others. (Philippians 2:4)

If you want to truly experience hope and happiness in your life, the best thing you can do is help someone else. I know that sounds counterintuitive, but it works.

Taking the focus off yourself and looking for ways to bless others takes your mind off your own problems, and as you give hope through words or acts of service, you receive a harvest of everything you give multiplied many times over.

When a farmer plants seeds in a field, he receives back an entire crop that provides for his family and so many others. God's promise that we will reap what we sow still amazes me. If we want something, we can start by giving that very thing away to others.

Today's Thought

True happiness comes when you actively live to bless another.

Dig Deeper into God's Word: Study Matthew 7:12; Galatians 6:2

Confident, Stable, and More than a Conqueror

Therefore, my beloved brothers and sisters, be steadfast, immovable, always excelling in the work of the Lord. (1 Corinthians 15:58)

The Word of God tells us that we are more than conquerors (see Romans 8:37). I believe that means we are assured of victory even before we have a problem.

Victorious becomes our new identity as children of God. We don't need to live with a victim mentality because we are confident that in the end, we always win. Being fully convinced of our victory in Christ allows us to be stable and calm, even in the midst of difficult circumstances.

The apostle Paul said we can be people who are steadfast, immovable, and always abounding in the work of the Lord. What a great description of what it means to follow Jesus! This is exactly how a person who has made God the foundation of his life can live.

Today's Thought

When you have confidence that God is in control, you are anchored and secure, because your hope is in the Lord.

Dig Deeper into God's Word: Study Deuteronomy 20:4; Psalm 108:13

Examples to Encourage

Jesus Christ is [eternally changeless, always] the same yesterday and today and forever. (Hebrews 13:8)

The Word of God is full of examples of fallible, imperfect people we can relate to. Their stories are recorded in the Bible to teach and encourage us.

Think about it: David got discouraged. Moses lacked confidence. Elijah got depressed. Gideon was afraid. Sarah laughed in disbelief at God's promise. The Israelites rebelled.

The men and women in the Bible weren't all some sort of superheroes—they were real people with real problems, just like you and me.

The next time you're discouraged or doubting yourself, just remember that God can help you the same way He helped the men and women of the Bible. He is the same yesterday, today, and forever!

Today's Thought

God doesn't help us because we are good—He helps us because He is good.

Dig Deeper into God's Word: Study Hebrews 6:17–18; Psalm 102:25–28

Remember What God Has Done

When I remember You on my bed, I meditate and thought-fully focus on You in the night watches, for You have been my help, and in the shadow of Your wings [where I am always protected] I sing for joy. (Psalm 63:6–7)

There are many instances recorded in the Bible when God instructed His people to remember, recount, and recall His mighty acts and the things He had done for them. When they failed to do so, they lost their appreciation, became selfish, and always went back into bondage.

Remembering the good things in life is certainly helpful and keeps us on the happy path of gratitude.

The simple fact is that thankful people are happy people, and happy people are often healthier than sad, discouraged, and hopeless people. Remember what God has done for you in the past, and allow that knowledge to give you hope for the future.

Today's Thought

Write down one thing each day that you are thankful for, and see how long your list can get before you run out of things God has done for you.

Dig Deeper into God's Word: Study Psalm 77:11; 1
   Corinthians 11:24–25

A Righteous Spirit

That which is born of the flesh is flesh [the physical is merely physical], and that which is born of the Spirit is spirit. (John 3:6)

How you feel about yourself in your spirit (heart) is a determining factor in your life. It sets the stage for all of your relationships, including your relationship with God. It affects your confidence, your courage, and your levels of peace and joy.

You can go backward or you can go forward—it depends on how you feel about yourself in your spirit.

The righteousness of God is yours through Christ Jesus. It is a gift God gives to those who accept Jesus as their Savior, and it is the condition our spirits must be in if we are to properly fellowship with God. In your quiet time with God, meditate on the fact that you are accepted and loved because of the work Jesus has done on your behalf.

Today's Thought

Jesus died so we might stand boldly before God and not shrink back in fear or shame.

Dig Deeper into God's Word: Study Micah 6:8;
    Romans 6:13–14

Cooperating with God

But without faith it is impossible to [walk with God and]
please Him, for whoever comes [near] to God must [neces-
sarily] believe that God exists and that He rewards those
who [earnestly and diligently] seek Him. (Hebrews 11:6)

Many people make the mistake of becoming passive, assuming that
good things will mysteriously happen without their cooperation.
But that is just not true. We are partners with God, and as such, we
must cooperate with Him.

There are many things we need to think about, say out loud, and
do on purpose. This is what it means to put your faith into action.

Our lives can come into agreement with God, but that won't
happen by accident. It is something that must be done purposefully
and relentlessly. Be diligent in your commitment to following God's
ways, and you will see good fruit in your life.

Today's Thought

When you do what you can, God will step in and do what
only He can do in your life.

Dig Deeper into God's Word: Study Proverbs 10:4–5;
    Proverbs 13:4

Busy or Fruitful?

Walk in a manner worthy of the Lord [displaying admirable character, moral courage, and personal integrity], to [fully] please Him in all things, bearing fruit in every good work and steadily growing in the knowledge of God [with deeper faith, clearer insight and fervent love for His precepts]. (Colossians 1:10)

Everyone today seems to be busy. Ask just about anyone how they are, and they will respond, "Busy." But we are making a mistake if we equate being busy with being fruitful.

For many years, I thought the busier I was, the more God would be pleased with me. The truth was, the busier I was, the less time I had to even hear from God concerning what His will was for me. It took me a while to learn to do less in order to achieve more.

In your quiet time with God, ask Him to give you the wisdom to schedule your day and your week according to His plan. Don't do things just to do them. Walk in obedience, and look to invest your time and energy into things that will have lasting impact for you and for others.

Today's Thought

God never called us to be busy; He called us to bear good fruit.

Dig Deeper into God's Word: Study Luke 10:41–42; Colossians 3:1

Creating an Atmosphere Where God Can Work

Set your mind and keep focused habitually on the things above [the heavenly things], not on things that are on the earth [which have only temporal value]. (Colossians 3:2)

Our thoughts, words, and attitudes create an atmosphere. It can be hectic and stressful, or it can be calm, positive, and even enjoyable. Thoughts become words, attitudes, body language, facial expressions, and even moods—and all of these things affect the atmosphere we live in.

God responds to our faith, our confident expectation that He is working on our behalf. If we have a negative situation, but a positive attitude, it opens the door for God to work and change our negative situation around.

God's desire for us is that we learn to live with a positive attitude—an attitude of faith and hope. No matter what our circumstances, our minds belong to us, and no one should do our thinking for us. Be passionate about being positive, and watch how God will work in your situation.

Today's Thought

A positive attitude and expectation of God lifts us above our circumstances and enables us to have peace in the midst of the storm and to have joy regardless of what is going on around us.

Dig Deeper into God's Word: Study Psalm 92:1–2;
    Hebrews 13:15–16

Made for a Unique Purpose

There is a glory and beauty of the sun, another glory of the moon, and yet another [distinctive] glory of the stars; and one star differs from another in glory and brilliance.
(1 Corinthians 15:41)

God created us all uniquely different. Like the sun, the moon, and the stars, God made us to be different from one another, and He has done it on purpose. Each of us has an individual destiny, and we are all part of God's overall plan.

Be secure in your uniqueness, knowing that God loves you and took great care in creating you. We never have to be threatened by the abilities of others. We can be free to love and accept ourselves and one another without feeling pressure to compare or compete.

If we attempt to be just like someone else, not only do we lose ourselves, but we question God's plan. God wants you to joyfully run your race; He doesn't want you feeling pressured to run someone else's race or fit into everyone else's plans. Different is more than okay; it is God's purpose for your life.

Today's Thought

You were fearfully and wonderfully made by the Creator of the universe. Never question your worth. You are special and unique in His sight.

Dig Deeper into God's Word: Study Psalm 139:14;
    Romans 12:6–8

Seasons Will Pass

Many hardships and perplexing circumstances confront the righteous, but the Lord rescues him from them all. (Psalm 34:19)

God has promised to never leave you or forsake you. He is always with you! There will be times in your journey when you will have to press forward, with just you and God. Those are trying times, but if you push through any discouragement, you will come out on the other side more rooted and grounded in God. You will develop a deep walk with Him that will be amazing.

However, if you give up, you'll get stuck in despair. The Bible tells us many hardships come against the righteous, but God rescues us from them all. When you are going through trying times, just remember they will not last forever. They come in seasons, and seasons will pass. In your quiet time with God, ask Him for the strength to keep going, and remember that you are never alone.

Today's Thought

There is one simple principle to overcoming every challenge you face: Don't give up! And remember: This too shall pass.

Dig Deeper into God's Word: Study Deuteronomy 31:6; 2 Corinthians 13:11

Excited about Your Life

That is why I remind you to fan into flame the gracious gift of God, [that inner fire—the special endowment] which is in you through the laying on of my hands [with those of the elders at your ordination]. (2 Timothy 1:6)

If you are a Christian, are you excited about it? Or have you become so accustomed to the idea of God's presence in your life that you have lost your zeal and enthusiasm?

God once spoke to my heart that I should always live amazed and not let the things that once excited me about my life in Christ become part of a mundane routine. And I think that is a good message for all of us.

Paul told Timothy to stir himself up, to fan the flame and rekindle the embers of the fire he once had. This is great advice. Don't let the things that once amazed you—your salvation, God's unconditional love, His daily provision, and an overcoming life—become mundane. Choose to wake up each day amazed and excited about your life and your ongoing relationship with God.

Today's Thought
Think about how privileged you are to be a child of God.

Dig Deeper into God's Word: Study 1 Samuel 2:1; Mark 1:22

Teach Your Mind to Work for You

Be transformed and progressively changed [as you mature spiritually] by the renewing of your mind [focusing on godly values and ethical attitudes], so that you may prove [for yourselves] what the will of God is, that which is good and acceptable and perfect [in His plan and purpose for you]. (Romans 12:2)

Did you know that your mind can work either *for* you or *against* you, depending on how you train it? When it works for you, it helps you stay positive, reach your goals in life, and think the kinds of thoughts that please God and enable you to enjoy each day. When it works against you, it can make you negative and discouraged and keep you from accomplishing what you want or need to do.

Our actions are the result of our thoughts. I often say, "Where the mind goes, the man follows." Make the intentional decision that you will begin to think faith-filled, positive thoughts based on God's Word. Developing the habit of thinking the way God wants you to will take time. Receive God's mercy when you make mistakes, and be determined to remain diligent and always ask for God's help. Your mind can go to work *for* you instead of against you and become a powerful, positive tool in your life.

Today's Thought

Choose your thoughts carefully, because they are containers for power. It is up to you whether that power is positive or negative.

Dig Deeper into God's Word: Study Philippians 4:8–9;
        Ephesians 4:22–24

Release the Weight of Worry

Do not be anxious or worried about anything, but in everything [every circumstance and situation] by prayer and petition with thanksgiving, continue to make your [specific] requests known to God. (Philippians 4:6)

It is one thing to know that we shouldn't worry, but it is quite another to actually stop worrying. One of the things that will help you let go of worry is to realize how utterly useless it is. Let me ask you some questions:

- How many problems have you solved by worrying?
- How much time have you spent worrying about things that never even happened?
- Has worry ever added to your peace, joy, or energy?

Of course not! The instant you begin to worry or feel anxious, remember that it is useless and give your concern to God. Release the weight of it and totally trust Him to either show you what to do or to take care of it Himself.

Today's Thought

Entrusting everything to God in prayer is your most powerful weapon to battle worry.

Dig Deeper into God's Word: Study Proverbs 12:25; Isaiah 43:1–3

Meditating on God's Word

But his delight is in the law of the Lord, and on His law [His precepts and teachings] he [habitually] meditates day and night. (Psalm 1:2)

All of the successful people we read about in the Bible had a habit of meditating on God's Word. They knew that it was the way to keep their minds renewed to God's ways. To meditate is simply to roll something over and over in your mind, to mutter it softly or speak it out loud.

Meditating on God's Word is very powerful. I like to look at meditating on God's Word like chewing my food. If I swallow my food whole, I don't get all of the nutrition that is in it. If we skim over God's Word or just hear a weekly sermon in church, it is like swallowing it whole and never getting the fullness of the good things out of it that God wants us to have.

The Word of God has inherent power, and I believe that power is best released as we think on it over and over.

Today's Thought

Don't meditate on today's problems—meditate on God's promises.

Dig Deeper into God's Word: Study Proverbs 2:2–5; John 6:63

God's Power at Work

But the free gift is not like the offense. For if by the one man's offense many died, much more the grace of God and the gift by the grace of the one Man, Jesus Christ, abounded to many. (Romans 5:15 NKJV)

God always gives us the grace to do what He asks us to do; however, He won't give us the grace to live outside of His will. If He's telling us not to do something that we decide to do anyway, we'll experience the pain of frustration and disappointment.

God gives us grace to match His call on our lives. When we do our own thing, we do it in our own strength. When we follow His leading, He always supplies the grace and the energy to do what He's called us to do.

The best part is that while we do have to choose to receive God's grace, we don't have to do anything to earn it. It's a free gift. When you choose to follow God's call, you can be confident that God will supply everything that you need to do it.

Today's Thought

Being in God's will is the most comfortable place to be.

Dig Deeper into God's Word: Study Jeremiah 10:12–13; Psalm 147:4–5

Living in Supernatural Favor

For You, O Lord, bless the righteous man [the one who is in right standing with You]; You surround him with favor as with a shield. (Psalm 5:12)

There is a distinction between natural favor and supernatural favor. Natural favor must be earned in order to receive it, but supernatural favor is a gracious and divine gift from God.

A perfect example of this is the life of Esther. God raised her up out of obscurity to become the queen of the entire land. He gave her favor with everyone she met, including the king. When an attack was planned against the Israelites, Esther went before the king in confidence to save her people, trusting she had God's favor.

Like Esther, we can move with the freedom and confidence that comes from living in God's favor. Regardless of the circumstances that come into your life, move forward in boldness and faith, knowing you have the supernatural favor of God. I believe in confessing God's Word out loud, so I suggest that each day you confess that you have the favor of God on your life.

Today's Thought

God's favor opens doors and provides opportunities for you that no one else can.

Dig Deeper into God's Word: Study Job 10:12;
        Proverbs 3:3–4

Prayer Is a Conversation

The sheep that are My own hear My voice and listen to Me;
I know them, and they follow Me. (John 10:27)

Prayer is more than us telling God what we want or need—prayer is meant to be a conversation. In your quiet time with God, make sure to listen to what He tells you. Either through His Word or as a direct revelation to your heart (which will always line up with the Word of God), God uses many ways to speak to you if you'll listen.

Like any conversation, time with God should involve talking and listening. I am convinced that we don't do nearly enough listening. You may have to develop an ability to listen, but God has some very awesome things to say. Learn to quietly wait on Him.

Let me remind you today that God lives inside of us. He is our constant companion. He is not someone we should talk to only when we have a need, but we should communicate with Him all throughout the day. As you do, it will help you build an intimate friendship with Him that will make your life awesome.

Today's Thought

God has invited us into a relationship of fellowship with Him. It is to be an intimate relationship in which we share absolutely everything.

Dig Deeper into God's Word: Study Jeremiah 29:12;
    Psalm 17:6

We Win in the End

*He who is in you is greater than he (Satan) who is in the
world [of sinful mankind]. (1 John 4:4)*

Most of us would agree that we are living in very difficult times
among many sinful and confused people, and we should be more
careful than ever before to not let our emotions take the lead role
in our lives.

Instead of being quick to become angry or being fearful of the
times we live in, we can take the Bible's advice to be as wise as ser-
pents and as gentle as doves (see Matthew 10:16).

In other words, we can be spiritually mature, patient, kind, and
gentle with others and wise enough to know that no matter what
happens, God will have the final say. It doesn't matter how bleak
things appear in the world; there is no darkness that can overcome
the light of God within us. Remember, God knows the end from the
beginning. He is in control. We can take peace and comfort in that
truth.

Today's Thought

*The world is dark, but in Christ, you are full of light, so be sure
to shine brightly today and every day.*

Dig Deeper into God's Word: Study Romans 8:37–39;
1 John 5:4–5

How to Think about People

Treat others the same way you want them to treat you.
(Luke 6:31)

How we think about people when we are not with them determines how we will treat them when we are. I really want to please God concerning how I make people feel, and I am sure you feel the same way. Our thoughts play a vital role in our being able to do that, and they greatly affect our relationships with people.

There is great benefit to positive, on-purpose thinking about others. We don't have to try to think about things we don't like (those thoughts come to our minds uninvited), but we can give them no entrance by choosing to focus on the good.

When you have your time with God, spend some of it thinking about the people you will be with that day. Instead of pondering all their faults and things you don't like about them, purposely think of the good things. This will help you treat them the way you would want to be treated.

Today's Thought

People don't always remember what we say, but they do remember how we made them feel.

Dig Deeper into God's Word: Study Romans 12:3;
    Galatians 5:22-23

God Thinks about You

Many, O Lord my God, are the wonderful works which You have done, and Your thoughts toward us. (Psalm 40:5)

Perhaps it never occurred to you that God thinks about you, but He does. God's thoughts toward us are found in His Word. His Word reveals His will. His Word is His thoughts written down for us to see.

Psalm 139 is a beautiful psalm by David that teaches us a great deal about how God views us: "How precious also are Your thoughts to me, O God! How vast is the sum of them! If I could count them, they would outnumber the sand. When I awake, I am still with You" (Psalm 139:17–18).

David declares that God's thoughts toward him (and us) are so many that they are like grains of sand on the beach. And guess what? They are good thoughts! God loves you, and you are always on His mind.

Today's Thought

You are never out of God's sight or off of His mind. He loves you and has a great plan for your life.

Dig Deeper into God's Word. Study Zephaniah 3:17; 1
    John 4:16

Cracked Pots

Yet, O Lord, You are our Father; we are the clay, and You our Potter, and we all are the work of Your hand. (Isaiah 64:8)

God doesn't require us to be perfect—He made us, and He knows we're human and will make mistakes. Our job is to get up every day and do our best to serve God with the gifts He has given us. We'll make mistakes, and when we do, we can receive God's forgiveness and move on.

God (the Potter) uses cracked pots (that's us) to do His work. We are containers God fills with His love and goodness to share with the world around us.

Don't be afraid of your flaws. Acknowledge them and allow God to use you anyway. Stop worrying about what you're not and give God what you are. Keep your eyes on God, who is perfect, and what He can do in you and through you.

Today's Thought

God knew every mistake you would ever make before you made them, and He loves you anyway.

Dig Deeper into God's Word: Study Isaiah 29:16;
    Psalm 119:73

Stable and Mature in Christ

I will not be enslaved by anything [and brought under its power, allowing it to control me]. (1 Corinthians 6:12)

Many people have convinced themselves that they are overly emotional people. They say, "I can't help it. My emotions get the best of me." If you've ever felt that way, let me tell you that you can be stable and mature in Christ. You don't have to be a victim of your emotions.

No one is "just emotional"; we may have chosen to allow ourselves to be led by our emotions until doing so became a habit, but with God's help we can change. God has given us a spirit of discipline and self-control, but we have to use it.

God gave you emotions so you could feel good and bad things, but He never intended those feelings to rule you. With God's help, you can discipline your mind, your will, and your emotions. You can be a stable and mature Christian who follows God and not your emotions.

Today's Thought

God has given us free will, and we can exercise it to make choices that line up with His will for our lives.

Dig Deeper into God's Word: Study 1 Corinthians 14:20; Ephesians 4:14–15

Accepting Yourself

*He must search for peace [with God, with self, with others]
and pursue it eagerly [actively—not merely desiring it].
(1 Peter 3:11)*

A lot of people really don't like themselves. They reject themselves.
But if we don't get along with ourselves, we won't get along with
other people. When we reject ourselves, we may feel that others
reject us as well.

How we feel about ourselves is a determining factor in our success in everything we do, including our relationships, and relationships are a vital part of our lives. God wants us to be confident and
accept that we are created by Him, and He doesn't make mistakes.

God loves us, and He wants us to accept His love. And because
of His love, we can love ourselves in a healthy, balanced, biblical
way. We are God's children—people who are loved, accepted, and
by His grace improving daily.

Today's Thought

*Our self-image is the inner picture we carry of ourselves.
Let your picture be based upon what the Word of God says
about you and nothing else.*

Dig Deeper into God's Word: Study Romans 9:20; Song
   of Solomon 4:7

Don't Be Afraid to Fail

For a righteous man falls seven times, and rises again.
(Proverbs 24:16)

It isn't possible to find out God's plan for your life without making a few mistakes along the way. The history books are filled with stories of great men and women who did incredible things, but prior to their achievements, they failed along the way.

Thomas Edison tried two thousand experiments before he successfully invented the light bulb. Abraham Lincoln lost several elections before he became president of the United States. We wouldn't have heard of either of these men if they had quit before they achieved success.

God has created us to keep moving toward His plan for our lives. He wants us to face new challenges, try new things, experiment, and be creative. Don't be afraid when you fail—your success may be right around the corner.

Today's Thought

The fear of failure is one of the biggest fears people have to confront if they intend to fulfill their purpose in life.

Dig Deeper into God's Word: Study Romans 5:3–4;
    Psalm 37:23–24

Diligent Prayers

The heartfelt and persistent prayer of a righteous man (believer) can accomplish much [when put into action and made effective by God—it is dynamic and can have tremendous power]. (James 5:16)

Many times, when we think of power, we think of something that happens quickly, with almost miraculous speed and force. But the power of prayer is not determined by whether or not results come instantly or dramatically.

In fact, James 5:16 teaches us that one way tremendous power becomes available is when we pray persistently. That means it will take some time and determination not to give up.

Be patient and trusting when you pray, and believe that the answer will come at just the right time if what you are praying is the will of God. If it isn't God's will, then expect Him to give you something even better.

Today's Thought

Prayer opens the door for God to get involved in every area of our lives and of those we pray for.

Dig Deeper into God's Word: Study Colossians 4:2; Luke 18:1

The Ongoing Work of God in Your Life

I am convinced and confident of this very thing, that He who has begun a good work in you will [continue to] perfect and complete it until the day of Christ Jesus [the time of His return]. (Philippians 1:6)

We want things to be done quickly in our lives, but God wants them to be of high quality, so He takes His time in training us. There are no overnight sensations in the kingdom of God. The things He is doing in your life right now have a twofold purpose: They are providing for you today, and they are preparing you for tomorrow.

Consider this: David's encounter with the lion and the bear prepared him for his battle against Goliath. Joseph learned how to lead in an Egyptian prison, learning lessons he would use when he was promoted to be second only to Pharaoh.

Don't be in too much of a hurry. If you go too fast, you will miss important lessons that come through the seemingly small decisions and events of each new day lived in relationship with the Lord. God is doing valuable things in our lives every day, and we can learn to recognize them if we trust Him in the process.

Today's Thought

If God gave us everything we asked for at once, we wouldn't be equipped to handle it. This is why God blesses, instructs, and guides us little by little.

Dig Deeper into God's Word: Study 1 Corinthians 4:5; Ephesians 4:11–13

Waiting with Hope

*And now, Lord, for what do I expectantly wait? My hope
[my confident expectation] is in You. (Psalm 39:7)*

Hope is not something we must wait to feel in order to have it. It is
something we can decide to have no matter how difficult our circumstances may seem. God promises that if we will become prisoners of hope, He will restore double our former blessings to us
(see Zechariah 9:12; Isaiah 61:7).

In other words, if you are willing to be locked up with hope to
the point where you are so hopeful that no matter what happens
you cannot stop hoping, then God will restore anything that you
have lost in your life and give you a double blessing.

Life is filled with negative situations, but we don't have to let
them make us negative. Hope is always positive, expecting something good to happen at any moment. While you are waiting for
your breakthrough, study God's Word and remember the good
things God has done for you in the past.

Today's Thought

*Hope in God is not merely wishing things would turn out
well; it is a powerful force that produces breakthroughs
when we diligently hold on to it.*

Dig Deeper into God's Word: Study Psalm 37:7–9;
    Psalm 27:14

Jesus Did It All

In whom we have boldness and confident access through faith in Him [that is, our faith gives us sufficient courage to freely and openly approach God through Christ]. (Ephesians 3:12)

No matter how hard we try or how much we do, we can never *do* enough good things to earn God's approval and acceptance. That may sound frustrating and defeating, but it is actually good news when we realize that Jesus has done all that needs to be done, and nothing we can ever do will improve on the job He did. The life, death, and resurrection of Jesus was enough for you and for me.

True rest comes when we are able to say, "I don't have to do anything to get God to love and accept me." We should do our best because we love God, and not in order to get Him to love us.

As believers, we can come before God because of all that Jesus did and realize that we stand before God "in Christ," not in ourselves. We have access to the throne of God's grace because of the blood of Christ, not because of anything we can ever do. Jesus is always enough!

Today's Thought

Your relationship with God isn't based on what you do, but on what Jesus has done for you.

Dig Deeper into God's Word: Study John 17:3; 1 John 5:20

Handling a Loss

The Lord is near to those who have a broken heart, and saves such as have a contrite spirit. (Psalm 34:18 NKJV)

Loss can be a very difficult part of life, and it is one we all experience. The good news is there is something waiting for you on the other side of loss. It may be a different job, a new relationship, or a new ability to empathize with others who are going through a situation similar to yours.

By God's grace, you can move through your loss and come out on the other side. The decision to move forward doesn't eliminate the emotions that we feel, but the emotions will subside as time goes by. Emotions run high when we are in any kind of pain, and it is best not to make rash decisions or sudden changes while we are hurting.

Instead, wait patiently on the Lord, and trust Him to help you make the decision to move through the loss and come out on the other side better, not bitter.

Today's Thought

Pain, suffering, and loss aren't the end of your story. There are still more chapters to be written.

Dig Deeper into God's Word: Study Psalm 147:3; Matthew 5:4

Faith over Fear

Be anxious for nothing, but in everything by prayer and supplication, with thanksgiving, let your requests be made known to God; and the peace of God, which surpasses all understanding, will guard your hearts and minds through Christ Jesus. (Philippians 4:6–7 NKJV)

Fear and anxiety are enemies we often face. If there is an area of your life where you are afraid, give that fear to God and receive His grace to enable you to have faith in that area.

For example, if you would love to apply for a position that would be a promotion in your company, but you've felt too fearful to do so, step out and try it. Even if you don't get the position, you will have been successful in stepping out in faith, and that is the most important thing.

In your quiet time with God, study and meditate on His Word about being free from fear and secure in Him. His Word will renew your mind, and fear will turn to faith and courage. Take the steps of faith that God leads you to take even though you might still feel some fear, and as you go forward you will begin to sense more and more freedom.

Today's Thought

With God's help, you can defeat fear and anxiety one step at a time. Take a step today.

Dig Deeper into God's Word: Study Jeremiah 1:8;
    Psalm 56:11

Rejoice, Rejoice

*Rejoice in the Lord always [delight, take pleasure in Him];
again I will say, rejoice! (Philippians 4:4)*

Serious and painful things happen at times in our lives, and we
need to be aware of them and prepared to face and deal with them.
But at the same time, because of the Spirit of God in our lives, we
can learn to relax and take things as they come without getting
nervous and upset about them. We can enjoy our lives even in the
midst of imperfection.

With God's help, we can learn how to be at peace, enjoying
the wonderful life He has provided for us through His Son, Jesus
Christ. Twice in Philippians 4:4, the apostle Paul tells us to rejoice.
He urges us in the following verses not to fret or have any anxiety
about anything but to pray and give thanks to God *in* everything—
not *after* everything is over.

We can rejoice in the middle of *any* challenging situation. In
spite of all the troubling things going on around us in the world,
our daily confession can be, "This is the day the Lord has made; we
will rejoice and be glad in it" (Psalm 118:24 NKJV).

Today's Thought

*Pay more attention to your blessings than you do to your
problems.*

Dig Deeper into God's Word: Study Isaiah 61:10;
    Psalm 113:1

Follow God's Lead

The Lord is my Shepherd [to feed, to guide and to shield me], I shall not want. (Psalm 23:1)

If we want to reach our goals or find success in life, it is essential that we follow God's lead.

There will always be people who offer us advice. Some of it may be good, but much of it may not. Or it may be good advice but simply at the wrong time, or it may be advice that will not work for us. It's important that we always look to God first and listen for His guidance and instruction.

God has created us as unique individuals, and He does not lead all of us in the same way. God has a different, unique, individual plan for each of us. So, if you want to win your race, you will need to find your own running style.

Of course, we can learn from other people, but we dare not try to copy them at the cost of losing our own individuality. Appreciate the advice and example of others, but in your quiet time with God, ask Him for His guidance and follow the promptings He gives you.

Today's Thought

The best guidance you will ever receive is the direction and guidance of the Holy Spirit.

Dig Deeper into God's Word: Study Isaiah 58:11;
    Proverbs 1:2–7

The Joy of Obeying God's Word

*For I shall delight in Your commandments, which I love. And
I shall lift up my hands to Your commandments, which I
love; and I will meditate on Your statutes. (Psalm 119:47–48)*

It brings great joy when we gratefully receive God's promises for
our lives and obey His commands. When we believe the Word of
God and obey whatever the Holy Spirit puts in our hearts to do, we
are destined to be overcomers in life. Believing God's Word delivers us from frustration and struggling, and we rest in the promises
of God.

The Word says, "For we who have believed (adhered to and
trusted in and relied on God) do enter that rest" (Hebrews 4:3
AMPC). If your thoughts have become negative and you are full of
doubt, it may be simply that you have become weary and stopped
believing God's promises. As soon as you start believing God's
Word, your joy will return and you will be at ease again. Thankfully, that place of rest in God is where He wants you to be *every
day* of your life.

Today's Thought

*Anytime you start to feel tense or anxious, remind yourself that God will fight your battles as you enter His rest
through faith.*

Dig Deeper into God's Word: Study John 14:23;
Deuteronomy 5:33

The Courage to Pursue Your Dreams

Yet in all these things we are more than conquerors and gain an overwhelming victory through Him who loved us [so much that He died for us]. (Romans 8:37)

God gives us dreams for the future, but sometimes those dreams can seem impossible. That's when fear starts to set in.

If you are determined to never give up on your dreams, then you have to take chances—you have to be courageous. Courage is not the absence of fear; it is pressing forward when you feel afraid. So when you face situations that threaten or intimidate you, pray for God's grace to give you boldness and courage so you can move ahead in spite of the obstacles you face.

The spirit of fear will always try to keep you from going forward. But you can defeat fear, because you are more than a conqueror through Christ who loves you.

Today's Thought

Don't shrink back when adversity arises. Stand firm, trusting God and knowing He is right there with you.

Dig Deeper into God's Word: Study 1 Corinthians 16:13; 2 Chronicles 32:8

Enjoying the Differences
of Others

With all humility [forsaking self-righteousness], and gentleness [maintaining self-control], with patience, bearing with one another in [unselfish] love. (Ephesians 4:2)

It's easy to expect everyone to be like us or be as we think they should be. But God wants us to enjoy the people He has put in our lives, not judge and criticize them.

In your quiet time with God, ask Him to help you form a habit of finding the good in people, not their flaws.

Everyone has faults, and we are called to be patient and long-suffering with them. If there are people in your life who have habits or mannerisms different from yours, learn to appreciate those differences. God has made them unique, just as He has made you unique. Don't forget that people have to overlook some of your behaviors, too.

This is the only way we can have peaceful, happy relationships. We must all practice being patient and adaptable.

Today's Thought

Don't waste your energy trying to change other people. Let God change the things that need to be changed.

Dig Deeper into God's Word: Study 1 Corinthians 12:4; Song of Solomon 6:9–10

Something to Look Forward To

*Such hope [in God's promises] never disappoints us, because
God's love has been abundantly poured out within our hearts
through the Holy Spirit who was given to us. (Romans 5:5)*

I think we all need things to look forward to. It may be a good meal
after a hard day's work, or it may be your yearly vacation. But the
things we look forward to motivate us to keep going in life. God
wants to do good things for each of us, and He wants us to enjoy
our life.

Always stay full of hope, for it is the confident expectation of
good. Look forward to and expect good things in your life. Abraham hoped against hope. He hoped when there was no physical
reason to hope. Looking to your circumstances won't always give
you reason to hope. But you can look beyond them to God's Word
and remember what He has done in your past and what He promises to do in your future.

Today's Thought

*We don't have to wait for our circumstances to change to
enjoy life, because as long as our thoughts are hopeful, we
will have joy in our hearts.*

Dig Deeper into God's Word: Study Proverbs 23:18;
Micah 7:7

A Healthy Mind Contributes to a Healthy Life

Finally, believers, whatever is true, whatever is honorable and worthy of respect, whatever is right and confirmed by God's word, whatever is pure and wholesome, whatever is lovely and brings peace, whatever is admirable and of good repute; if there is any excellence, if there is anything worthy of praise, think continually on these things [center your mind on them, and implant them in your heart]. (Philippians 4:8)

There is a proven connection between the mind and the body, and it gives us an easy and inexpensive way to help maintain good health. You can choose to think positive, peaceful, biblical thoughts in order to develop a healthier spirit, soul, and body.

Nobody wants to be a victim, and we certainly don't want to be victimized by our own thoughts. Learning to think purposely and aggressively, instead of passively providing an empty space for whatever thoughts come to mind or the devil offers, is the way to become the victor instead of the victim.

In your quiet time with God, ask Him to help you think faith-filled thoughts, and get started today on your way to a healthier mind and body.

Today's Thought

Instead of focusing on what is wrong, set your mind on what is right: the good things God has done in your life.

Dig Deeper into God's Word: Study 3 John 1:2; 1 Timothy 4:8

Fully Convinced of God's Promises

But he did not doubt or waver in unbelief concerning the promise of God, but he grew strong and empowered by faith, giving glory to God, being fully convinced that God had the power to do what He had promised. (Romans 4:20–21)

The Bible states that Abraham was "fully convinced" concerning the promise of God; he did not waver or doubtingly question. In other words, he had set his mind and was able to keep it set during temptation.

You will be tempted; that's just a fact of life. But with God's help, you can resist temptation. The Bible says we are to be on our guard, and that means we should watch out for the things the devil uses to derail our faith in God.

People who have set their minds will stick with their decisions, realizing that they have to make it through the difficult times in order to get the result they desire. Setting your mind on things above (see Colossians 3:2) means being firm in your decision to agree with God's ways of living no matter who or what may try to convince you that you are wrong.

Today's Thought

Make up your mind ahead of time that you are going to go all the way through with God.

Dig Deeper into God's Word: Study Exodus 14:14; Isaiah 41:13

Make a Thankful List

O give thanks to the Lord, for He is good; for His compassion and lovingkindness endure forever! (Psalm 107:1)

To help you achieve and maintain a new level of contentment in your life, I encourage you to use some of your quiet time with God to make a list of everything you have to be thankful for. It should be a long list, one that includes little things as well as big things. Why should it be long? Because we all have a lot of things to be thankful for if we just look for them.

Get out a piece of paper and start listing things you have to be thankful for. Keep the list and add to it frequently. Make it a point to think about the things that you're grateful for when you're driving the kids to an activity or waiting in line at the post office or whatever you may be doing throughout the day. You can only learn the power of thankfulness by practicing it every day. Meditating on what you have to be grateful for every day and verbalizing it will be amazingly helpful to you.

Today's Thought

The next time you have lunch or coffee with a friend, be intentional about talking about the things you are thankful for instead of recounting all of your problems.

Dig Deeper into God's Word: Study 1 Thessalonians 5:18; Hebrews 12:28–29

Living Freely and Lightly

*Walk with me and work with me—watch how I do it. Learn
the unforced rhythms of grace. I won't lay anything heavy
or ill-fitting on you. Keep company with me and you'll
learn to live freely and lightly. (Matthew 11:28–30 MSG)*

Living freely and lightly in the "unforced rhythms of grace" sounds
good, doesn't it? I'm sure you have had enough heavy stuff in your
life. I have, too, and I want to live freely. It's nice to know that with
God, we don't have to worry about things, figure everything out, or
carry the burdens in our lives.

It is refreshing to realize that we don't need to know everything
about everything. We can get comfortable with saying, "I don't
know the answer to this dilemma, and I'm not going to worry about
anything because God is in control, and I trust in Him. I'm going to
rest in Him and live freely and lightly."

Worry isn't restful at all. In fact, it steals rest and the benefits of
rest from us. So next time you feel you are carrying a heavy burden
in your mind or find yourself worried or anxious, remember you
can live freely and lightly with God's help.

Today's Thought

*When we're overloaded with the cares of life, we can take a
mental and emotional vacation.*

Dig Deeper into God's Word: Study 1 Peter 5:7;
    John 14:27

Learning to Be Content

*Not that I speak from [any personal] need, for I have
learned to be content [and self-sufficient through Christ,
satisfied to the point where I am not disturbed or uneasy]
regardless of my circumstances. (Philippians 4:11)*

The Bible teaches us to be content no matter what our circumstances may be. Contentment is a decision to be happy with what
you already have. Unfortunately, we usually learn to be content by
living discontented lives for a long time and then finally saying,
"Lord, I don't want to live this way any longer." But it doesn't have
to be that way.

You can choose to be content every day, starting today. It isn't
wrong to want things or to want your life to change, but we should
be content where we are while we are getting to where we want
to be.

When we want something so much that we feel we cannot
be happy without it, then it has stopped being a desire and has
become a lust. Things don't have the power to keep us happy for
very long, but God can give us a contentment that surpasses our
understanding.

Today's Thought

*Sometimes we ask God for what we want, and He gives us
what we need.*

Dig Deeper into God's Word: Study 1 Timothy 6:6–8;
    Hebrews 13:5

Bolder Prayers

Therefore let us [with privilege] approach the throne of grace [that is, the throne of God's gracious favor] with confidence and without fear, so that we may receive mercy [for our failures] and find [His amazing] grace to help in time of need. (Hebrews 4:16)

Not only can we go to God in prayer during our quiet times with Him, but we can pray boldly, which means without fear and unreservedly.

Jesus has made a way for us to approach God with boldness because He made us righteous through His death on the cross. Because of what He has done for us, we can go to God with total confidence and pray unashamedly, knowing that He loves us, hears us, and will answer our prayers in the best way possible.

Jesus has made us worthy, and when we approach God boldly, we can count on Him to be merciful to us. Mercy means that God doesn't punish us as our sins deserve, and He blesses us in ways that we don't deserve to be blessed—if we are bold enough to ask.

Today's Thought

Ask God for what you want and need, and trust Him to give you what is best at the right time.

Dig Deeper into God's Word: Study John 15:7;
    Matthew 21:22

Discovering God's Best

Every good thing given and every perfect gift is from above;
it comes down from the Father of lights [the Creator and
Sustainer of the heavens], in whom there is no variation
[no rising or setting] or shadow cast by His turning [for He
is perfect and never changes]. (James 1:17)

God loves you, and He wants to have a deep, intimate, personal relationship with you. He loves you so much that He sent His Son, Jesus, so you could enjoy the very best life He came to offer.

God does not play favorites (see Acts 10:34), and every promise in His Word applies to you as much as anyone else. Yes, you can receive the blessings, favor, peace, and joy that come as a child of God. If you trust God and follow Him wholeheartedly, you will discover your best life in Him.

God has a great purpose for you, and I urge you to not settle for anything less. He wants to bless you and give you a life that will not only thrill you but also fulfill you and bring you deep joy and sweet satisfaction. It will also challenge you, stretch you, and help you discover that, in Christ, you can do more than you have ever imagined.

Today's Thought

Jesus came that you might have and enjoy life to the fullest.

Dig Deeper into God's Word: Study Proverbs 16:3;
    Psalm 138:8

God Hears Your Prayers

First of all, then, I urge that petitions (specific requests), prayers, intercessions (prayers for others) and thanksgivings be offered on behalf of all people. (1 Timothy 2:1)

When you are praying for someone else (intercession), don't be disappointed if you don't see changes right away. Your prayer opens the door for God to work, but it may take a while before the person you pray for is ready to listen. If you start to get discouraged, take some time and thank God that you believe He is working even though you may not see any evidence yet.

It is a wonderful thing to stand before God and pray for someone who doesn't know how to pray for themselves or who needs more prayer power than what they can generate praying alone. Sincerely praying for another is one of the best gifts you can give them.

I encourage you not only to pray for others but also to ask God to cause people to pray for you. We all need people to come alongside of us in prayer, because we are stronger together than we are individually.

Today's Thought

Jesus intercedes for us (see Romans 8:34), and we can join Him in His ministry of intercession by praying for others.

Dig Deeper into God's Word: Study Romans 8:26; Ephesians 6:18

Resurrection Power

And this, so that I may know Him [experientially, becoming more thoroughly acquainted with Him, understanding the remarkable wonders of His Person more completely] and [in that same way experience] the power of His resurrection [which overflows and is active in believers]. (Philippians 3:10)

I have found that the more experience I have with God, the easier it becomes to trust Him in every situation life brings. Being a Christian is about a lot more than making a weekly trip to church; it's about learning to do life with God. He wants to be included in all that you do, and when He is, you will experience a new power flowing through you and in your life.

We have the same power in us that raised Christ from the dead (see Romans 8:11), so obviously we should not live defeated lives. Even though we face many trials in life, we can overcome, and in the process we will experience God in new ways that will help us understand how wonderful He is.

Today's Thought

God's resurrection power lives in you!

Dig Deeper into God's Word: Study Psalm 121:1–8;
    Ephesians 3:20

Go with God's Plan

The steps of a [good and righteous] man are directed and established by the Lord, and He delights in his way [and blesses his path]. (Psalm 37:23)

When life isn't going the way we thought it might, it's easy to try to take over and tell God what He needs to do. God doesn't follow our plans, but we should follow His. Sometimes our plan is to take a route that is quick and easy, but God chooses one that is long and hard. When that happens, it is difficult for us to understand, but we eventually learn that God's plan is the best one.

We live life forward, but often we only understand it as we look back. What you despise right now may end up being one of the best things you could have gone through. I have gone through many difficult things in my life, just as I am sure many other people have, but they truly have made me a better person.

Continue to let God guide your steps, no matter how difficult it is, because they will lead you to the right destination.

Today's Thought

Peace of mind comes with trusting that God's will is better than ours, even when we don't yet understand it.

Dig Deeper into God's Word: Study Proverbs 15:22; Psalm 119:105

The Gift in You

For just as in one [physical] body we have many parts, and
these parts do not all have the same function or special
use, so we, who are many, are [nevertheless just] one body
in Christ, and individually [we are] parts one of another
[mutually dependent on each other]. (Romans 12:4–5)

You may look at the development of potential as something only for
those who have some special talent, and you may not see yourself
as being one of them. But God's Word assures us that we all share
in the gifts that God gives.

You may not be a painter, singer, designer, speaker, or author,
but you are something—you have unique gifts and abilities. And
whatever you are is important to God and to the rest of us.

The Bible teaches us that even though our gifts vary, like the different parts of our physical bodies, we are all mutually dependent
on one another. Every person's part is a great contribution if they
use it for the glory of God.

Today's Thought

You don't have to be someone else, but you do need to be
fully *you.*

Dig Deeper into God's Word: Study 1 Peter 4:10–11;
    Proverbs 18:16

Law and Grace Can't Be Mixed

For the Law was given through Moses, but grace [the unearned, undeserved favor of God] and truth came through Jesus Christ. (John 1:17)

Many New Covenant believers still live under the Old Covenant, or they mix the old with the new. They have some grace and some law, but in reality they have neither one. Grace and law can't be mixed.

The law demands that we work to keep it. It requires sacrifice on our part when we fail. The apostle Paul taught that works of the flesh and grace could not be mixed, or both become useless.

Grace is Jesus Christ working, and law is man working. God does not need our help to save us. We can live by faith, through which we receive God's grace, instead of living by trying to keep the law in order to soothe God's anger.

Today's Thought

You are accepted, loved, and approved before God because of the sacrifice of Jesus on your behalf.

Dig Deeper into God's Word: Study Romans 3:28; Galatians 2:16

Learning to Rest in God's Plan

Commit your way to the Lord; trust in Him also and He will do it. (Psalm 37:5)

You can simplify your life by learning to develop trust in God. Far too often, we don't live in peace or rest, because we haven't allowed ourselves to trust Him.

Maybe your trust has been betrayed by people too many times in the past and it has made you afraid to trust anyone, or maybe you're just a very independent person. Even so, it is critical to learn to trust God.

It's easy to get stressed-out and worn-out physically, trying to deal with life on your own, but there is a better way. Jesus said that if those who labor and are heavily burdened would come to Him, He would give them rest and would ease, relieve, and refresh their souls (Matthew 11:28).

God's way is best!

Today's Thought

Even when it doesn't appear to make sense, trust God and experience His freedom and rest.

Dig Deeper into God's Word: Study Matthew 6:25–26; Proverbs 16:9

Renewing Your Strength

But those who wait for the Lord [who expect, look for, and hope in Him] will gain new strength and renew their power. (Isaiah 40:31)

Isaiah teaches us to wait for the Lord when we know our strength needs to be renewed. Waiting for God means spending time with Him in His Word and His presence.

There are certain people we can draw strength from just by being around them. Their very presence, the way they talk and approach life, seems to make us feel better when we are discouraged. Likewise, there are others who seem to make us feel worse. They have a way of putting a negative edge on things.

When you need to be strengthened, I encourage you to spend time with God and with people who will point you to Him. Spending time in God's presence is like sitting in a room filled with sweet-smelling perfume. If we sit there long enough, we take the fragrance with us everywhere we go.

Today's Thought

Lasting strength and courage come only from the Lord. Wait for His direction, His peace, and His strength to propel you forward.

Dig Deeper into God's Word: Study Psalm 46:1–3;
    Isaiah 26:3–4

The Answer to the Sin Problem

Since all have sinned and continually fall short of the glory of God, and are being justified [declared free of the guilt of sin, made acceptable to God, and granted eternal life] as a gift by His [precious, undeserved] grace, through the redemption [the payment for our sin] which is [provided] in Christ Jesus. (Romans 3:23–24)

Sin is a problem for everyone, but Jesus is also the answer for everyone. No problem is really a problem as long as there is an answer for it.

Not only have we fallen short of the glory of God, but according to Romans 3:23, we are currently falling short. This indicates it is a continual problem, yet Jesus is continually at the right hand of the Father, making intercession for us, so this continual problem of sin has a continual and uninterrupted answer.

Although we deal with sin, we don't have to focus on our failures. When we are convicted of sin, we can admit it, repent, and then turn toward Jesus. By focusing on Him and His Word, we will receive the power to overcome.

Today's Thought

God's Word teaches us to turn away from all that will distract us unto Jesus, who is the author and finisher of our faith (see Hebrews 12:2).

Dig Deeper into God's Word: Study 1 John 1:6–10; Luke 5:31–32

Receiving the Help of
the Holy Spirit

But when He, the Spirit of Truth, comes, He will guide you into all the truth [full and complete truth]. For He will not speak on His own initiative, but He will speak whatever He hears [from the Father—the message regarding the Son], and He will disclose to you what is to come [in the future].
(John 16:13)

As Christians, we can receive the daily guidance of the Holy Spirit. When Jesus ascended to sit at the right hand of the Father, He sent the Holy Spirit to represent Him and act on His behalf.

The Holy Spirit is present in our lives to teach us, pray through us, convict us of sin, and convince us of righteousness. He is present to lead and guide us in all matters of daily life, both spiritual and practical.

The Holy Spirit is your ever-present help. He is referred to as "the Helper" (see John 14:26). Fortunately, Jesus didn't leave you alone to fend for yourself. He sent the Holy Spirit to help you in every area of your daily life.

Today's Thought

In your quiet time with God, thank Him for the gift of the Holy Spirit and ask Him to help you follow His leading.

Dig Deeper into God's Word: Study Psalm 32:8;
    Psalm 25:4–5

Accepted, Not Rejected

The Lord is on my side, He is among those who help me;
therefore I will look [in triumph] on those who hate me.
It is better to take refuge in the Lord than to trust in man.
(Psalm 118:7–8)

Jesus did not enjoy the acceptance or approval of most people while He was on earth. He was despised and rejected by men. But He knew His heavenly Father loved Him. He knew who He was, and it gave Him confidence.

Everything that Jesus endured and suffered was for our sake. He went through rejection so that when we face it, we too can go through it and not be damaged by it, or if we have already been damaged, then we can completely recover.

There will always be some people who will not accept you, but their acceptance isn't what ultimately matters. God loves you unconditionally; He approves of you and accepts you. That is all the acceptance you will ever truly need.

Today's Thought

Knowing that you are loved and accepted by God can help you live boldly and without fear.

Dig Deeper into God's Word: Study Ephesians 5:29–30; John 6:37–39

Confident in Who God
Made You to Be

*But by the [remarkable] grace of God I am what I am, and
His grace toward me was not without effect. (1 Corinthians
15:10)*

Truly confident people resist the temptation to compare themselves with others. No matter how talented, smart, or successful we
are, there is always someone who is better at a particular thing, and
sooner or later we will run into them.

I believe confidence is found in realizing the gifts we have and
appreciating that they are unique. Then we boldly do the best we
can with what God has given us to work with. Confidence is never
found in comparing ourselves with others and competing with
them.

Real joy is not about being better than someone else, but in
being the best we can be for the Lord. Always struggling to maintain the number one position is hard work. In fact, it's impossible.
So instead of looking at those around you, look up and keep your
focus on God.

Today's Thought

*Security and confidence come from knowing you are cre-
ated by God for a purpose and embracing the person He
has created you to be.*

Dig Deeper into God's Word: Study Proverbs 3:26; 2
    Corinthians 7:16

The Key to Godly Success

Commit your works to the Lord [submit and trust them to Him], and your plans will succeed [if you respond to His will and guidance]. (Proverbs 16:3)

If you want to do anything amazing with your life, you will have to learn to work with God and wait on Him. Achieving success requires firm faith, not wishful thinking.

It is good to have God-given dreams, but understand that it takes time for those dreams to develop fully. In your quiet time with God, pray for a dream that is even greater than what you have now, but also pray that you enjoy each step of your journey and that you will realize that success requires an investment of time and lots of hard work.

Many people never fulfill their destiny because they are not willing to pay the price up front. They settle for something less than the best God has in His plan for them, because they don't want to do the hard things or take risks. Don't let that be you! Dream big. Follow God and be willing to do whatever He asks you to do.

Today's Thought

Step out and find out what God wants you to do, and you won't live with regrets.

Dig Deeper into God's Word: Study Jeremiah 10:23; Deuteronomy 28:1

What God Can Do in a Moment

The Lord is my strength and my [impenetrable] shield; my heart trusts [with unwavering confidence] in Him, and I am helped; therefore my heart greatly rejoices, and with my song I shall thank Him and praise Him. (Psalm 28:7)

The Christian life isn't always lived on the mountaintop; there are days you still have to go through the valley. But as a child of God, there is something especially encouraging you need to remember today: *God can do more in one moment than you can do in a lifetime.*

There is no situation that intimidates Him. There is no mess, no dysfunction, no abuse, no pain that He can't heal. One word from God, one moment in His presence, one touch of His hand can change the entire course of your life.

Don't be discouraged when things don't go well. You have the Creator of the universe on your side. You serve God, who can do the impossible. And He can do it in a moment.

Today's Thought

Your past, your limitations, your obstacles are no match for the power of God.

Dig Deeper into God's Word. Study Matthew 19:26; Job 42:2

When God Seems Silent

Search me [thoroughly], O God, and know my heart; test me and know my anxious thoughts; and see if there is any wicked or hurtful way in me, and lead me in the everlasting way. (Psalm 139:23–24)

David sometimes asked God to examine him to see if anything was in his heart that was not right. This is a bold step, but one that clearly proves whether or not a person truly wants God's will, no matter what it might be.

When it seems God is silent, it is possible there is something blocking us from hearing Him—a sin, a wrong attitude, or a misunderstanding on how to hear from God.

We don't need to be afraid to know the truth, because it will set us free. In your quiet time with God, ask Him to examine your heart, just like David did. Whatever God shows you will be for your benefit and will help you continually draw closer to Him.

Today's Thought

A healthy, close relationship with God requires asking Him to reveal truth to us and a willingness to change when He asks us to.

Dig Deeper into God's Word: Study John 8:47; Jeremiah 33:3

Allowing for Mystery

Oh, the depth of the riches and wisdom and knowledge of God! How unsearchable are His judgments and decisions and how unfathomable and untraceable are His ways! (Romans 11:33)

God promises to give us insight into mysteries and secrets as we seek Him (see Ephesians 1:9, 17), and yet we are also told by the apostle Paul that we only know "in part," and we won't know all things until we are with Jesus, face-to-face (1 Corinthians 13:9–10).

Trust requires unanswered questions. God reveals many things to us and gives us answers to complex problems, but there are times when we could not receive the answer to a situation even if God gave it. Our finite minds aren't capable of grasping some things that only God knows.

It is one thing to trust God when things are going our way and we understand everything, but it is quite another to trust God when we don't fully understand why we are going through something. My opinion is that it requires a much greater faith to do the latter.

Today's Thought

There is beauty in trusting God and putting your faith in Him in all seasons of your life.

Dig Deeper into God's Word: Study Psalm 37:3–6;
    Job 11:7–9

The Power of Mercy

For judgment will be merciless to one who has shown no mercy; but [to the one who has shown mercy] mercy triumphs [victoriously] over judgment. (James 2:13)

Mercy always triumphs over judgment. In other words, mercy is a greater thing than judgment. I doubt that any of us can show others much mercy unless we have truly realized the depth of our own frailty, weaknesses, and mistakes and learned to receive mercy from God.

When we realize how much mercy God gives us each and every day, it makes us generous in giving mercy to others.

In your quiet time with God, take a few minutes and ponder if there is anyone in your life who you need to extend mercy to. Mercy is a gift. It cannot be earned or deserved, but when it is freely given, people experience the power of God's love in a practical way that often changes them.

Today's Thought

We need no other reason to show mercy to others than the fact that God has and does show us mercy.

Dig Deeper into God's Word: Study 1 Peter 2:9–10; Matthew 5:7

Dealing with Jealous People

The fear of man brings a snare, but whoever trusts in and puts his confidence in the Lord will be exalted and safe. (Proverbs 29:25)

Not everyone is going to be happy when you begin a new life in God and begin to live in His plan for you. Your new attitude, new mindset, and new blessings can cause others to be convicted of sin and jealous of the things they are lacking in their own lives.

And it's not just material things. As you follow God, there will be people who are jealous of your newfound peace, emotional health, and joyful outlook on life.

Don't apologize for what God has given you just because someone else is jealous of it. If they can't be happy for you, that is their problem, not yours. You can encourage and pray for them, but don't let their jealousy discourage you. Rejoice in the blessings of the Lord

Today's Thought

Make a choice not to let the accusations of jealous or suspicious people intimidate you into giving up what God has provided.

Dig Deeper into God's Word: Study Proverbs 27:4;
    Ecclesiastes 4:4

Opportunity Brings Opposition

A wide door for effective service has opened to me [in Ephesus, a very promising opportunity], and there are many adversaries. (1 Corinthians 16:9)

Every time God puts a new idea in our hearts or gives us a dream, vision, or new challenge for our lives, the enemy will be there to oppose us.

God constantly calls us to new levels. Some seem big and important; others seem relatively small or insignificant. Whatever the case, when we reach a new level with God, we will face a new level of opposition from our enemy, the devil.

Along with opposition, however, comes opportunity. And God is always with us, so we have no need to fear. Some things may seem too great for us, but nothing is impossible with God. He is not surprised or frightened by anything, and with Him, we can accomplish any challenge set before us.

Today's Thought

If you are determined to reach the new levels God is calling you to, then don't give up in the face of opposition.

Dig Deeper into God's Word: Study Jeremiah 32:17; 1 Timothy 6:12

Your Debt Is Paid

If we [freely] admit that we have sinned and confess our sins, He is faithful and just [true to His own nature and promises], and will forgive our sins and cleanse us continually from all unrighteousness [our wrongdoing, everything not in conformity with His will and purpose]. (1 John 1:9)

God doesn't expect us not to make mistakes. He already knows about every mistake we will ever make, and He has already decided to forgive us. Sin does have to be paid for, but we don't have to pay. Jesus already paid for our sin.

What if when you went to the electric company to pay your bill, they looked up your account and said, "Someone paid your bill in full yesterday." How foolish would it be if you kept standing there trying to pay the bill that had already been paid?

That's exactly what we do sometimes concerning our sin. We ask God to forgive us, and He does, and yet we keep trying to pay with feelings of guilt. In our quiet time with God, we can learn to ask and receive. Asking for forgiveness is one step, but receiving it completes the process.

Today's Thought

Stop trying to pay a debt that Jesus has already paid for.

Dig Deeper into God's Word: Study Psalm 51:1–2;
  Romans 3:23–25

A New View of God

*But God clearly shows and proves His own love for us, by
the fact that while we were still sinners, Christ died for us.
(Romans 5:8)*

Perhaps you need an entirely new view of God—a biblical view, not
a worldly view, as many have today.

I can assure you that no matter what you have done or what you
may be doing wrong, God does love you, and although He will ask
you to change, He has never stopped and never will stop loving you.

If you receive His love right in the midst of your imperfection, it
will empower you to change your ways with His help. Fear does not
help us truly change. It may provoke us to control our behavior for
a time, but unless we are changed inwardly, we will never change
permanently; only God can give us a new heart and a new nature
(see 2 Corinthians 5:17).

If we receive God's love even while we are still sinners, our gratitude for His great mercy will make us want to please Him rather
than be afraid of Him.

Today's Thought

*God is good, kind, merciful, slow to anger, forgiving, faith-
ful, and just.*

Dig Deeper into God's Word: Study Deuteronomy
     10:12; 1 John 4:7–12

God with Us

"Behold, the virgin shall be with child and give birth to a Son, and they shall call His name Immanuel"—which, when translated, means, "God with us." (Matthew 1:23)

Jesus came into the world so we could be redeemed from our sins, know God, and experience His very best in our lives. He wants to have close fellowship with us and to be invited into everything concerning us.

This is why one of the names of God, Immanuel, means "God with us." He wants to be with us, intimately involved in our lives. He wants us to know His voice and follow Him.

God's will is that we hear clearly from Him. He does not want us living in confusion and fear. With God's help, we can be decisive, secure, and free. He wants each of us to fulfill our destiny and to walk in the fullness of His plan for us.

Today's Thought

God's gift to you is a new life filled with righteousness, peace, joy, and intimacy with Him.

Dig Deeper into God's Word: Study Romans 8:31; Jeremiah 1:19

Receiving the Word of God

And those [in the last group] are the ones on whom seed was sown on the good soil; and they hear the word [of God, the good news regarding the way of salvation] and accept it and bear fruit—thirty, sixty, and a hundred times as much [as was sown]." (Mark 4:20)

It is important that we receive the Word of God. Some hear the Word but don't actually receive it, and it does them no good. In Mark chapter 4, Jesus told a parable of a sower who sowed seed (the Word of God) into different kinds of ground, but only one type of soil bore fruit. The different kinds of ground represent the different types of hearers of the Word of God.

We are taught in this parable that even those who are willing to hear don't always hear fully or in the right way. They don't hear with the serious intent of truly receiving the Word they hear. They are emotional hearers who initially get excited, but when their faith is tested, they give up.

When the Word of God is genuinely and sincerely received, it has the power to do an amazing work in our souls. It renews our mind and changes us into the image of Jesus Christ. If you haven't had a genuine change of character, ask yourself if you are truly receiving the Word of God.

Today's Thought

The Word of God is alive and active. It will change you if you will truly receive it.

Dig Deeper into God's Word: Study Colossians 3:16;
    Psalm 119:10–11

This Is the Way

Your ears will hear a word behind you, "This is the way, walk in it," whenever you turn to the right or to the left.
(Isaiah 30:21)

We all need direction and guidance, especially in the face of a new situation. When facing a new challenge or circumstance, the first question to ask yourself is, "Is this God's will for me?" And the second question is, "Do I have inner peace about this?"

When our hearts are right and our motives are pure, we can trust God to provide everything we need each step of the way and fill us with peace as we move forward.

We follow God by taking one step of obedience at a time. As we take each step and see God working, we know it is safe to take another step. It is not wise to merely follow our personal desires, fears, emotions, or good ideas, or the advice of others. In your quiet time with God, ask for His direction. Acknowledge Him in all your ways, and He will direct your steps.

Today's Thought

The more you listen for God's leading and learn to follow Him, the easier it becomes to hear and follow Him.

Dig Deeper into God's Word: Study James 1:22; 2
    Timothy 3:16–17

Reject Self-Pity

"For I know the plans and thoughts that I have for you,"
says the Lord, "plans for peace and well-being and not for
disaster, to give you a future and a hope." (Jeremiah 29:11)

Self-pity is a destructive emotion. It blinds us to our blessings and
the possibilities before us, and it steals our hope for both today and
tomorrow. People who pity themselves often think, *Why should I*
try to accomplish anything? It won't make a difference.

Don't waste another day of your life in self-pity. When you lose
hope and begin to feel sorry for yourself, stop and say, "I refuse to
feel sorry for myself. I may be in a difficult season of life right now,
but I will not stop hoping for better things."

God has thoughts and plans for your good, to give you hope for
your future. If you hold on to your hope by keeping your focus and
faith in Jesus, amazing things will happen in your life.

Today's Thought

When we fall into self-pity, we are essentially rejecting God's
love and doubting His ability to change things.

Dig Deeper into God's Word: Study Romans 8:28;
2 Corinthians 4:16–17

The Choice Is Yours

Choose for yourselves this day whom you will serve. (*Joshua 24:15*)

The first step in doing anything is choosing to do it. In order to encourage someone, you first choose to look for the best. In order to be at peace, you first choose not to worry. In order to start something new, you first choose to step out and go for it.

You may not know how it's all going to work out, but you can make some foundational choices today. Begin by saying, *Today I choose peace over fear! Today I choose to break that old habit and start a good one! Today I choose not to lash out in anger! Today I choose not to live in the past!*

Make a choice, take a step, and never forget to ask for God's help (His grace) in executing your choice. We can do all things with and through Him, but we can do nothing without Him (see Philippians 4:13).

Today's Thought

You don't always get to choose what happens around you, but you do get to choose how you will respond.

Dig Deeper into God's Word: Study John 15:5; 1 Kings 18:21

Setting a Godly Example

Be an example and set a pattern for the believers in speech, in conduct, in love, in faith, and in [moral] purity. (1 Timothy 4:12)

I am convinced that people believe more of what they see us do than what they hear us say. That's why it is important that we understand our responsibility to set a good, biblical example. How we live our faith is essential to being an effective witness for those around us.

Don't just tell others what they should be doing, but let them see you set the example. If a parent tells a child to be kind, and then the child sees their mom and dad being rude to one another, they have wasted their words.

The Bible says we should watch and pray (see Mark 14:38). In our quiet times with God, I think we need to watch ourselves a little more and pray we will live out the faith we so boldly profess. When we set the right example, it is a beautiful way to share our faith.

Today's Thought

Our actions speak so much louder than our words.

Dig Deeper into God's Word: Study Matthew 5:16; 1 Peter 1:14–15

Hope for the Future

Now faith is the assurance (title deed, confirmation) of
things hoped for (divinely guaranteed), and the evidence of
things not seen [the conviction of their reality—faith com-
prehends as fact what cannot be experienced by the physi-
cal senses]. (Hebrews 11:1)

When you think about the future, are you hopeful? Or do you
struggle with a sense of dread? People who have seen God's faithfulness in the past tend to be hopeful about the future. They know
a bad situation can turn into a powerful testimony.

Hope is the opposite of dread. A close cousin to fear, dread steals
the ability to enjoy everyday life and makes people anxious about
the future.

Hope allows us to trust God and leave our unanswered questions in His hands; it empowers us to remain at peace, and enables
us to believe the best about the days to come. When we live with
hope, we have a confident expectation that God is in charge and
that He is leading us into His great plan for our lives.

Today's Thought

You can live with hope, because God has the power to
provide for you and lead you through every situation. All
things are possible with God!

Dig Deeper into God's Word: Study 1 Peter 1:13;
    Proverbs 24:14

Do you have a real relationship with Jesus?

God loves you! He created you to be a special, unique, one-of-a-kind individual, and He has a specific purpose and plan for your life. And through a personal relationship with your Creator—God—you can discover a way of life that will truly satisfy your soul.

No matter who you are, what you've done, or where you are in your life right now, God's love and grace are greater than your sin—your mistakes. Jesus willingly gave His life so you can receive forgiveness from God and have new life in Him. He's just waiting for you to invite Him to be your Savior and Lord.

If you are ready to commit your life to Jesus and follow Him, all you have to do is ask Him to forgive your sins and give you a fresh start in the life you are meant to live. Begin by praying this prayer...

> *Lord Jesus, thank You for giving Your life for me and forgiving me of my sins so I can have a personal relationship with You. I am sincerely sorry for the mistakes I've made, and I know I need You to help me live right.*
>
> *Your Word says in Romans 10:9, "If you declare with your mouth, 'Jesus is Lord,' and believe in your heart that God raised him from the dead, you will be saved" (NIV). I believe You are the Son of God and confess You as my Savior and Lord. Take me just as I am, and work in my heart, making me the person You want me to be. I want to live for You, Jesus, and I am so grateful that You are giving me a fresh start in my new life with You today.*
>
> *I love You, Jesus!*

It's so amazing to know that God loves us so much! He wants to have a deep, intimate relationship with us that grows every day as we spend time with Him in prayer and Bible study. And we want to encourage you in your new life in Christ.

Please visit joycemeyer.org/KnowJesus to request Joyce's book *A New Way of Living*, which is our gift to you. We also have other free resources online to help you make progress in pursuing everything God has for you.

Congratulations on your fresh start in your life in Christ! We hope to hear from you soon.

Joyce Meyer is one of the world's leading practical Bible teachers. A *New York Times* bestselling author, Joyce's books have helped millions of people find hope and restoration through Jesus Christ. Joyce's programs, *Enjoying Everyday Life* and *Everyday Answers with Joyce Meyer*, air around the world on television, radio, and the Internet. Through Joyce Meyer Ministries, Joyce teaches internationally on a number of topics with a particular focus on how the Word of God applies to our everyday lives. Her candid communication style allows her to share openly and practically about her experiences so others can apply what she has learned to their lives.

Joyce has authored more than one hundred books, which have been translated into more than one hundred languages, and over 65 million of her books have been distributed worldwide. Bestsellers include *Power Thoughts*; *The Confident Woman*; *Look Great, Feel Great*; *Starting Your Day Right*; *Ending Your Day Right*; *Approval Addiction*; *How to Hear from God*; *Beauty for Ashes*; and *Battlefield of the Mind*.

Joyce's passion to help hurting people is foundational to the vision of Hand of Hope, the missions arm of Joyce Meyer Ministries. Hand of Hope provides worldwide humanitarian outreaches such as feeding programs, medical care, orphanages, disaster response, human trafficking intervention and rehabilitation, and much more—always sharing the love and gospel of Christ.

JOYCE MEYER MINISTRIES
U.S. & FOREIGN OFFICE
ADDRESSES

Joyce Meyer Ministries
P.O. Box 655
Fenton, MO 63026
USA
(636) 349-0303

Joyce Meyer Ministries—Canada
P.O. Box 7700
Vancouver, BC V6B 4E2
Canada
(800) 868-1002

Joyce Meyer Ministries—Australia
Locked Bag 77
Mansfield Delivery Centre
Queensland 4122
Australia
(07) 3349 1200

Joyce Meyer Ministries—England
P.O. Box 1549
Windsor SL4 1GT
United Kingdom
01753 831102

Joyce Meyer Ministries—South Africa
P.O. Box 5
Cape Town 8000
South Africa
(27) 21-701-1056

OTHER BOOKS BY JOYCE MEYER

The Power of Simple Prayer
Power Thoughts
Power Thoughts Devotional
Reduce Me to Love
The Secret Power of Speaking God's Word
The Secrets of Spiritual Power
The Secret to True Happiness
Seven Things That Steal Your Joy
Start Your New Life Today
Starting Your Day Right
Straight Talk
Teenagers Are People Too!
Trusting God Day by Day
The Word, the Name, the Blood
Woman to Woman
You Can Begin Again
Your Battles Belong to the Lord*

JOYCE MEYER SPANISH TITLES

Belleza en Lugar de Cenizas (Beauty for Ashes)
Buena Salud, Buena Vida (Good Health, Good Life)
Cambia Tus Palabras, Cambia Tu Vida (Change Your Words,
Change Your Life)
El Campo de Batalla de la Mente (Battlefield of the Mind)
Como Formar Buenos Habitos y Romper Malos Habitos
(Making Good Habits, Breaking Bad Habits)
La Conexión de la Mente (The Mind Connection)
Dios No Está Enojado Contigo (God Is Not Mad at You)
La Dosis de Aprobación (The Approval Fix)
Efesios: Comentario Biblico (Ephesians: Biblical Commentary)
Empezando Tu Día Bien (Starting Your Day Right)

Hágalo con Miedo (Do It Afraid)
Hazte Un Favor a Ti Mismo...Perdona (Do Yourself a Favor...Forgive)
Madre Segura de Sí Misma (The Confident Mom)
Pensamientos de Poder (Power Thoughts)
Sanidad para el Alma de una Mujer (Healing the Soul of a Woman)
Santiago: Comentario Bíblico (James: Biblical Commentary)
Sobrecarga (Overload)*
Sus Batallas Son del Señor (Your Battles Belong to the Lord)
Termina Bien Tu Día (Ending Your Day Right)
Usted Puede Comenzar de Nuevo (You Can Begin Again)
Viva Valientemente (Living Courageously)

BOOKS BY DAVE MEYER

Life Lines

* Study Guide available for this title